Ron Gannett

THE Jesus Passages

Exploring the Words of Jesus Through Journaling

The Jesus Passages
Exploring the Words of Jesus Through Journaling

Published by Deep River Books
Sisters, Oregon
www.deepriverbooks.com

ISBN – 10: 9781937756482
ISBN – 13: 1937756483

Library of Congress: 2012950300

Cover design by Joe Bailen, Contajus Designs

To Susie

Her love for Jesus brightens the passages of my life.

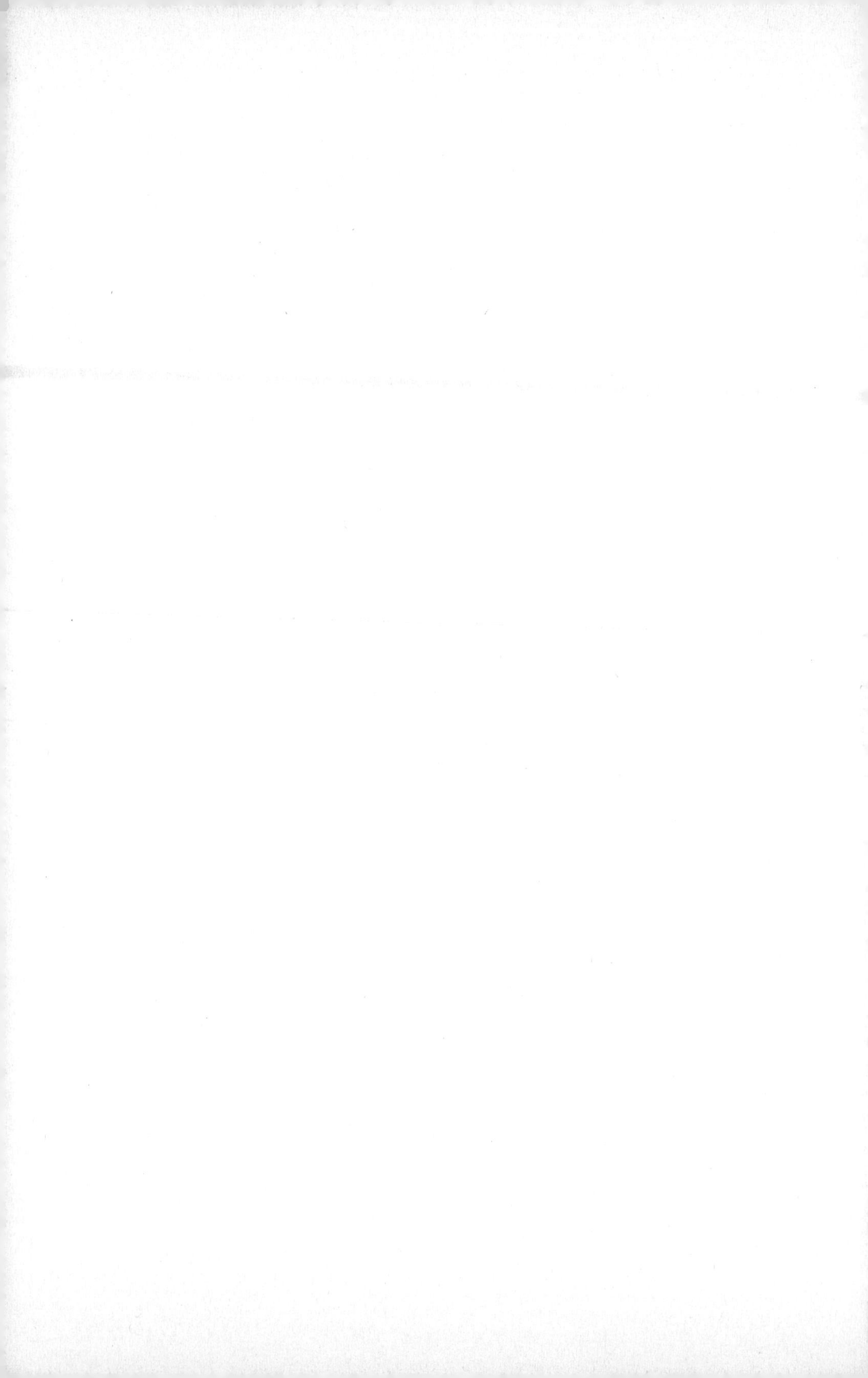

CONTENTS

GETTING ACQUAINTED

Welcome to a personal conversation with Jesus! You were created to enjoy an eternal relationship of life shared with Him. The Lord of heaven longs to walk alongside you to help fulfill your life purpose and to conquer daily challenges.

This relationship, like all others, blossoms when each person takes time to listen to the other in order to discover ways to grow together. Often Jesus hears people pray or talk about Him, but He knows that only listening to His words will ignite His glory in your life and bind a relationship like none other.

Too many followers of Jesus struggle simply because they do not know His words. They claim faith in Him but fail to listen and obey. This journal provides an environment where you can dialogue with Jesus to hear and respond to His eternal truth. You will discover that He can speak for Himself, and He will unveil the wisdom and hope you desperately need. Best of all, you will grow a love for the Savior, which will empower all you do.

Jesus shared His passion on His final night in the Upper Room when He reminded the disciples: "If you love me, you will obey my commands." Even during His physical absence, a relationship with Him could continue and deepen through simple obedience. He wanted them to know that the key to a fulfilling relationship depended on their response to His words.

As you walk through each Jesus Passage, don't be surprised if the reading for that day is timed perfectly for you. After all, He also promised that the Holy Spirit would teach and encourage you as you read His words. When Jesus speaks, you will learn how He answered many of the same challenges and hurts you endure. If you listen carefully, even His whispers will shout grace in your life.

The destination of this journey is to become more like Jesus. So, grab your Bible and use this journal to create an environment where He can teach you to be the person He designed you to be. After all, no invitation compares with this.

Come to me, all you who are weary and burdened, and I will give you rest. Take my yoke upon you and learn from me, for I am gentle and humble in heart, and you will find rest for your souls. For my yoke is easy and my burden is light.

MATTHEW *11:28–30*

WHO CAN USE THIS JOURNAL?

The *Jesus Passages* Journal is designed for almost any person or situation. There is flexibility for individual use, group study, or unique opportunities that arise. The simplicity of the Journal enables almost anyone to guide others in a purposeful discussion of each passage. Here are some suggested uses that might stimulate you to think of ways to enjoy the Journal.

Individuals

Many people enjoy the richness that develops in their walk with God by spending time alone in the Journal. Place it next to your Bible and walk through the Journal at your own pace. No matter how long it takes to complete the 267 passages, you will be anxious to do it again, comparing the insights you discover about Jesus each time through.

Couples

Couples are often looking for natural ways to foster their spiritual relationship. You can set a regular time to use the Journal together or do it separately with the intention of sharing your results with each other. This adventure will create an environment where meaningful conversations will occur. Create a schedule and watch God enrich your marriage.

Families

Parents have a desire to pass on the Christian faith to their children but often feel inadequate. The Journal is a tool that will introduce the entire family to the words of Jesus and create an atmosphere for spiritual conversation involving everyone. Families can use the Journal at the dinner table or reserve nights of the week to read it together. The Journal is user-friendly so that both parents and children can lead the sessions, empowering leadership and ownership. You will be surprised and refreshed by the transformation you will see in the family.

Small Groups

Many small groups in the church, neighborhood, or at work are looking for a tool that is easy to use for both the leader and participants. The Journal provides a biblical approach that stimulates discussion and life application. Group members can journal in private then gather to discuss their insights. Leadership can be rotated since the Journal guides everyone through the process. Groups can walk through the Journal chronologically or use the topical index in the back for focused study. Your group will never exhaust the insights they can discover in the words of Jesus.

Friends

You have people in your life who desire to know God better or have spiritual questions. The Journal provides these friends the opportunity to experience the words of Jesus for themselves in a way that begs for a response. The gift of a Journal may become the gift that keeps on giving by providing the fodder for spiritual conversations that help you both. Watch your discussions about the Journal develop a common bond that enriches your friendship.

Community Volunteers

People who serve in the community are often eager to find ways to bring a spiritual influence to those they serve. The Journal can be used in hospitals, jails, youth organizations, military services, assisted-care homes, or anywhere people long for help. The Journal's flexibility and simplicity enables it to fit most situations. With a little planning, you can discover a creative way to unleash the power of Jesus' words with the people you serve.

Teachers and Speakers

Whether you are a regular teacher or occasional speaker, the Journal offers you a wide range of topics and stimulating group questions. As a resource, it can be used in Sunday school classes, Bible studies, or devotional talks. The biblical focus and creative questions in the Journal will ease your preparation time while fostering personal application in the learners.

Topical Studies for Everyone

A topical index of the Jesus Passages is provided in the back of the Journal. Both individuals and groups will find the listings helpful to focus their study on a subject of personal interest. Leaders can create their own curriculum by selecting passages of interest for their family or group.

Discover resources for using the Jesus Passages in your home or group at www.readthebiblewithus.com.

THE JOURNAL FORMAT

Since the Journal is designed to foster interaction between you and the words of Jesus, the passages walk you through every episode chronologically in His life. The readings follow "A Harmony of the Gospels" found in the *NIV Study Bible*, with minor variations. Even though some episodes will tweak your imagination more than others will, they all contain significant lessons for life.

Each of the 267 passages follows the same format, and space is provided for you to record your insights. You will become the author of this book. Following these steps will help unfold the message God has for you.

STEP 1: *Read the Bible Passage*

Since reading the biblical story is essential to interacting with the words of Jesus, feel free to reread the passage until you have a basic understanding. Many of the passages have parallels in the other Gospels, which are also noted for those who desire further reading.

STEP 2: *Hook*

These questions help individuals or groups focus on the message presented in the Scripture passage being read. This process breaks the ice so that minds and hearts are better prepared to understand and discuss the biblical truth.

STEP 3: *Book*

Insights are provided to guide you toward a key idea in the episode in order to foster understanding. When *Italics* are used, it refers to a direct quote from the New International Version of the Bible. Since these comments are limited, you may find it helpful to have a study Bible or commentary on hand to answer additional questions.

STEP 4: *Took*

This final section contains questions that beg for a personal response to Jesus' words. Your goal is to record practical "takeaways" that will enrich your relationships with God and people you know. This is your opportunity to deepen your love for Christ by obeying His words. Be practical, personal, and specific.

TIPS FOR GETTING STARTED

The journey of a lifetime may begin with the first step, but it also requires continuous walking to arrive at the destination. Since every passage will open new vistas in your walk with Jesus, you will want to stay on the path to learn all you can. Periodically review these suggestions to help you maintain your focus and finish well.

- Experiment with your schedule to discover what time is best for regular use and enjoyment of the Journal.
- Feel free to journal at your own pace. Jesus will still be there if you get behind.
- Keep the Journal next to your Bible as a reminder. Dust is usually not a sign of success.
- Refuse to get bogged down in difficult portions of a biblical reading. Simply write about the truths you do understand.
- Read the journal slowly and allow time to meditate so that the Holy Spirit may have an opportunity to guide and teach you. Open your heart and be aware of holy nudges.
- Search for personal applications that will reshape your heart, mind, words, and actions. Remember that your love for God is reflected by your desire to become like Him.
- Share your Journal discoveries to encourage others. As you talk, you will stir your own passion for journaling and for what you are learning.
- Deal with moments of discouragement in life by rereading some of your past journaling in order to remember principles you previously discovered.
- Think legacy. One day, people you love will read the insights recorded in your Journal and be strengthened in their walk with God.

Enjoy the Journey!

THE *Early Years*

Passages 1–25

Passage 1

Was Jesus Some Last-Minute Solution?

Read: Genesis 12:1–3 and Galatians 3:6–9

Hook: When did you last witness something special in your life that made you feel God was at work in you?

Book: Talk about advance planning—look at this. The promise God made to Abraham, almost 2,200 years before the birth of Jesus, predicted a worldwide blessing. When the apostle Paul wrote to the church in Galatia, he declared that the life and death of Jesus was the fulfillment of this promise that brought God's blessing to those who believe. Only the God of love could care about you thousands of years before your own birth in order to provide what you really need!

Took: How does it embolden your walk with God when you realize that centuries in advance God planned to bless you?

PASSAGE 2

Can I Really Trust the Jesus Story?

READ: LUKE 1:1–4

HOOK: Why are some people so skeptical or antagonistic toward the Bible?

BOOK: Luke's introduction to his account of the Jesus Story for his Gentile readers used language that removed any doubt regarding authenticity. What did he say in this passage to make you feel confident about the historical record of the Lord Jesus?

TOOK: How does this Jesus Passage encourage a skeptic to probe further? What is the balance between certainty and faith?

Passage 3

Nuts in the Family Tree?

Read: Matthew 1:1–17 and Luke 3:23–38

Hook: Which of your relatives is the most unlike you?

Book: These two passages outline the genealogical record to verify that Jesus had a rightful claim to the throne of David—He is Messiah! What may seem like boring reading becomes exciting when you see some of the surprising names on the lists. Which people would you not expect on Jesus' family tree?

Took: How has God used your family background, both good and bad, to prepare you to love and serve Him?

Passage 4

God Slips into a Body

Read: John 1:1–18

❖

Hook: Why do you think God created people to live in human bodies?

Book: Don't let the human body of Jesus fool you—He is really God in that flesh. John introduced Jesus as the *Word* to remind you that He took on human flesh to reveal the Heavenly Father to us. As you read the passage, look for descriptions of both His deity and His humanity and weigh the significance of each.

Took: What can you discover about the Heavenly Father by simply observing the human life of Jesus?

Passage 5

A Woman's Worst Nightmare

Read: Luke 1:26–38 and Isaiah 7:14

Hook: Which personal hurt lingers in your head that you wish would just go away?

Book: Can you imagine the implications of an unplanned pregnancy for Mary in that culture? The message of the angel confirmed that this was no surprise to God. Mary was a key player in His plan to bless the world—even through her pregnancy! What impresses you about her response in verse 38?

Took: What possibilities do you see for God to take the surprises or bad stuff you are experiencing now to bring about good results for you and others?

Passage 6

Answer Life with the Bible

Read: Luke 1:46–55

Hook: How do people tend to respond to dramatic changes that interrupt the flow of their lives?

Book: Mary's reaction was remarkable as she embraced God's call on her life in spite of the hardship she encountered. She accepted God's choice as grace from heaven and responded with this song of praise. It contains at least fifteen quotes from the Old Testament, revealing how much the Word of God was loved and respected in Jewish homes like hers.

Took: Which one of these quotes could you use in your life or home at this time? Ask the Lord to do it!

Passage 7

Sacrifice Doesn't Always Hurt

Read: Matthew 1:18–19

Hook: Can you think of choices you make that benefit others but may hurt your reputation or relationships?

Book: Joseph's righteousness, or walk with God, controlled his response to this apparent scandal. Imagine the difficulty his family and friends must have had believing his story. He considered his options and took the one that was best for Mary, ignoring the personal cost to himself. How does Joseph remind you of Jesus?

Took: Which person or situation in your life needs a righteous and sacrificial response from you right now? What will you do?

Passage 8

Stain Removal

READ: MATTHEW 1:20–21

HOOK: Is the term "sin" cool? How would people respond today if you used that word in a conversation? Why?

BOOK: The angel informed Joseph that all these unusual events were unfolding for a grand purpose—*to save his people from their sins*. God set in motion a plan to solve the problem mankind could not resolve for themselves. Removing the barrier that separated the Father from His creation was a high priority in heaven since the stain of sin touches everything.

TOOK: Joseph understood the consequences of sin and willingly made the necessary sacrifice to free people from that bondage. What sacrifice could you make to heal or remove the stain of sin in a friendship or even in your own walk with God?

Passage 9

Closer Than You Think

Read: Matthew 1:22–25

Hook: When was the last time you wondered whether God really cared about your life or troubles? Why do you tend to feel so insignificant at times?

Book: No person is trivial to God. The meaning of *Immanuel* contains three small but powerful words: *God with us*!

God: Jesus is the Father's Son.

With: He came to live on earth.

Us: He came for you and for everyone who ever lives.

These three words reflect the lifestyle and teaching of Jesus, who invested His life in anyone who accepted Him. Just the anticipation of this truth stirred instant and complete obedience in Joseph.

Took: How does believing that Jesus is Immanuel, *God with us*, bring significance and motivation to your life?

PASSAGE 10

Set Your Clock by God's

READ: MICAH 5:2 AND GALATIANS 4:4–5

HOOK: Can you think of a time when God had you in the right place at the perfect time for something special to happen?

BOOK: Micah prophesied over seven hundred years before Jesus' birth the precise place He would be born—in the town of Bethlehem. The apostle Paul later wrote that the timing was perfect. The Heavenly Father ordered events before, during, and after the life of Jesus to fulfill His will through Christ. As you read the Jesus Passages, you will often see the Father speaking, caring, or guiding the process in some way.

TOOK: God's timing is perfect for you too! What is happening in your life right now that is a "God thing?" How could you be more sensitive to God's clock?

Passage 11

Seeing God in Strange Places

READ: LUKE 2:1–7

HOOK: When did you feel close to God in an unusual location?

BOOK: What a drama: Caesar's decree, family roots in the royal city of Bethlehem, journey for a pregnant Mary, taxes to pay, no room in the inn, and birth in a stable! These details are rich in significance, showing God's plan and provision for those who trust Him. Mary and Joseph learned to see God in the unique and even unwanted circumstances of life.

TOOK: How do you see God casting events in your life to unfold His plan or provision for you?

Passage 12

Reclaiming Your Joy

Read: Luke 2:8–14

⚜

Hook: Can you remember a day when you received some great news? Why was it so special?

Book: Do you sense the excitement in *good news of great joy*? The angel wanted people to know that God solved the greatest problem mankind ever had by providing a Savior. Only Jesus could uniquely fulfill this task because He is *Christ the Lord*—God Himself. His mission would bring both *glory to God* and *peace to men*. Only God's Son could bring the peace the world longs for, peace with God and with others.

Took: What is robbing you of your joy these days? How could you reclaim joy by letting Christ be the Lord in your life? Be specific.

PASSAGE 13

God Never Stutters

READ: LUKE 2:15–20

HOOK: What is the best advice you ever ignored?

BOOK: Even though being a shepherd was viewed as simple work, this group was anything but. They were smart enough to investigate what they had been *told*, to tell others what they had been *told*, and to praise God that they found things *just as they had been told*. They discovered deep joy by simply believing that the Words of God are always true and worthy of trust.

TOOK: People are often tempted to ignore God's teaching or to twist it to fit their personal situation or opinions. In which area of life do you trust in yourself instead of God's Word? How would reversing this bring joy into your life?

Passage 14

The Pause That Refreshes

Read: Luke 2:19 and Isaiah 9:6–7

Hook: When was the last time you paused to reflect on a significant event in your life?

Book: At times Mary paused to simply contemplate the events leading up to the birth of her special son, Jesus. It seems she wanted to wring every drop of meaning from the experience in order to fully appreciate it. Isaiah's prophecy provides a glimpse of what she saw: *Wonderful Counselor, Mighty God, Everlasting Father, and Prince of Peace!*

Took: Pause and ponder Jesus, the *Wonderful Counselor, Mighty God, Everlasting Father, and Prince of Peace*. Which of these descriptions do you need most today? Why?

PASSAGE 15

A Window on Your Soul

READ: LUKE 2:21–24

HOOK: Why do most people resist following instructions?

BOOK: The hearts of Joseph and Mary were publicly displayed in simple steps of obedience: following Jewish laws of circumcision, naming the child *Jesus*, complying with purification rites, and offering a sacrifice of consecration. The couple revealed deep personal devotion to God by refusing to allow their unique situation and poverty to prevent them from obeying His commands.

TOOK: What choices could you make to grant people a glance into your soul?

PASSAGE 16

Passion for the Right Stuff

READ: LUKE 2:25–32

⚜

HOOK: Describe the traits of the most passionate Christian you know.

BOOK: Simeon probably had all these traits and more. He was righteous and devout, patiently waited for God's promises to Israel, and was led by the Holy Spirit. His passion is self-evident in his prayer desiring Jesus to be a Light to the Gentiles and to bring glory to Israel as well. Simeon longed to see all people know that salvation comes from Jesus.

TOOK: Are your passions centered on the right things? How could you make Simeon's passion for the salvation of others a priority in your life?

Passage 17

No Time for Neutrality

Read: Luke 2:33–35

⸙

Hook: Why do people think they can be neutral about Jesus?

Book: Simeon prophesied that Jesus would be a divider of people. Some would *fall* in unbelief while others would *rise* in faith. Their response to Jesus would reveal their hearts. Mary would grieve when she witnessed the evil reaction to her son. Since even ambivalence is unbelief, every person will either accept or reject the Lord.

Took: Because there is no neutrality toward Jesus, what changes could you make to better demonstrate your allegiance to Him?

Passage 18

Faithfulness Opens Doors

Read: Luke 2:36–38

❈

Hook: Can you think of a time when God rewarded you for honoring Him in a specific way?

Book: Anna was a woman with a short marriage but a long record of faithfulness. Her reward for lifelong dedication in temple service was the opportunity to see the *Child* and glimpse the salvation of God. The Lord honored her eighty-four years of sacrifice and faithfulness with unexpected joy.

Took: Do you crave some joy? Since faithfulness is God's gateway to joy, which area of your life needs some authenticity? Prepare to be surprised.

PASSAGE 19

When People Think the Worst

READ: MATTHEW 2:1–6

HOOK: When was the last time you felt misunderstood or mistreated by others?

BOOK: King Herod was probably *disturbed* because he feared competition. If he had read the seven-hundred-year-old prophecy of Micah, the king would have known that Jesus was a different kind of King—who simply wanted to *shepherd His people*. Herod was reading his own evil motives into an innocent Jesus. Jealousy consumes and distorts reality.

TOOK: What should you remember when tempted to think the worst by calling someone's good "bad"?

Passage 20

Controlling People

Read: Matthew 2:7–12

Hook: How do you respond when a controlling person tries to manipulate you?

Book: King Herod's deception failed to work. When the Magi met the Christ child, they were so *overjoyed* that they spontaneously worshiped Him. The king's manipulation was even thwarted by God, who warned the Magi to take another route home. Manipulation will never control the purposes of God.

Took: Who are the controlling people in your life? What do the Magi teach you about responding to manipulation?

PASSAGE 21

Anger Management

READ: MATTHEW 2:13–18

HOOK: When did you last have an angry person hurt you in some way?

BOOK: King Herod's lust for power drastically interrupted the life of Mary and Joseph. Even though his anger turned their world upside down, God had prepared the family with this warning and the gifts of the Magi to support them on the road to Egypt. God's grace and supply was greater than Herod's anger and schemes.

TOOK: What advice should you give yourself the next time an angry person turns on you?

Passage 22

Sweet Dreams

Read: Matthew 2:19–23

❖

Hook: Why do you think your dreams often reveal some of your fears?

Book: This is the fourth dream provided by God to preserve the life of the infant Jesus. Dreams from God revealed His desire to guide their lives and remove all fears. To no one's surprise, every written or spoken word from God came true without exception.

You may not have angels speaking in your dreams, but, thankfully, you have the clarity and authority of God's Word to direct and protect you.

Took: Which area of your life is screaming for guidance from God's Word? Which fear would be relieved if you simply followed the words of the Heavenly Father?

Passage 23

No Place Like Home

Read: Matthew 2:23 and Luke 2:39–40

Hook: How did your upbringing prepare you for the challenges of life?

Book: The early years of Jesus were marked by disadvantages and turmoil. Later, people would sneer and call him a *Nazarene* because He came from a humble, insignificant town. Yet, under the loving and godly leadership of Joseph and Mary, He matured physically and spiritually.

Even though your surroundings may seem overwhelming or wanting, never underestimate the impact of a God-honoring home.

Took: What would distinguish a house from a home? How could your home become an environment where people would be encouraged to love and obey the Lord?

Passage 24

Balancing Dual Responsibilities

Read: Luke 2:41–51

❧

Hook: Can you think of a time when your walk with God brought you into conflict with someone?

Book: Even at the young age of twelve, Jesus knew that He had two spheres of responsibility since He was God's Son as well as the son of Mary and Joseph. This episode reveals the tension of this dual responsibility. In spite of any questions or misunderstandings Mary may have harbored, she *treasured* these events in her heart, while Jesus was *obedient* to His earthly parents. Evidently, they all worked at balancing their dual authorities in life.

Took: Divine and human authorities both have a call on your life too. How does this tension exist, and what could you do to bring balance?

PASSAGE 25

Jesus the Teenager

READ: LUKE 2:52

HOOK: How would you describe the highs and lows of your teen years?

BOOK: Jesus needed personal development like any other young person. What little is known about His early years is summarized in four statements that describe His maturing process: *wisdom* (mental), *stature* (physical), *favor with God* (spiritual), and *favor with man* (relational). One can safely assume that He *grew* in these four areas to prepare for life and ministry.

TOOK: Why would these four topics provide a potential outline for a self-help book? Which of the four do you need to work on most? What advice do you think Jesus would give you?

Beginning of Public Ministry

Passages 26–40

Passage 26

The Big Turn

Read: Matthew 3:1–6, See also Mark 1:1–6 and Luke 3:1–6

Hook: How do you tend to justify your shortcomings or sins?

Book: Evidently, God doesn't accept self-serving excuses. The dramatic dress, diet, and message of John the Baptist screamed that repentance must be done God's way. He reminded people of the prophet Elijah (2 Kings 1:8), who warned Israel to repent of personal evil to avoid God's judgment. Like Elijah, John's message proclaimed that everyone, no matter how good or religious they thought they were, must repent. Real faith turns from sin and chooses to love and follow Jesus.

Took: Have you ever made a conscious decision to repent of your sin before God and commit to follow Jesus? Take time to write a prayer to either initiate or renew this commitment of faith in Jesus. God invites you to repent by making "The Big Turn."

PASSAGE 27

Hollow Apologies

READ: LUKE 3:7–20, SEE ALSO MATTHEW 3:7–12 AND MARK 1:7–8

HOOK: When was the last time you heard an insincere apology? Why do people waste the words when they don't mean it?

BOOK: No matter who was in the audience, John neither minced his words nor watered down his call for genuine change. He challenged people to go beyond words to *produce fruit in keeping with repentance*. Genuine faith is visible. John's urgency anticipated the coming of Jesus, whose judgment would separate people like wheat from chaff based on their repenting faith. This message eventually cost John his freedom and his life.

TOOK: Can you think of a friend whose repentance seems hollow to you? What could you do to be a John the Baptist in this person's life?

PASSAGE 28

Humility Pays

READ: MATTHEW 3:13–17, SEE ALSO MARK 1:9–11 AND LUKE 3:21–23

HOOK: Why is humility so difficult?

BOOK: Even though Jesus was superior to John, He submitted to the Father's will through baptism. In this humble act, Jesus identified with John's righteous message of repentance and was rewarded with ringing endorsements by both the Holy Spirit and the Heavenly Father. God honored His Son's obedience by personally introducing Him to the world.

TOOK: God is waiting to honor your humility as well. Which situation in your life would change dramatically if sprinkled with submission and humility?

Passage 29

Beating Temptation

Read: Matthew 4:1–11, See also Mark 1:12–13 and Luke 4:1–13

⁂

Hook: What would you name as the top three temptations most people wrestle with and why are these so tempting?

Book: The strategies of Satan have not changed. He catches you at a weak moment (Jesus was fasting and hungry). The devil provokes you to violate the truth you know and guides you down a path to honor him at God's expense. Jesus beat the tempter at his own game by simply applying God's Word to every temptation. God has not left you in the dark but provides His Word to enable victory over any temptation.

Took: Do you want to kick a personal temptation? Practice the example of Jesus by identifying your biggest temptation and writing down some Bible verses that will empower you to be free.

Passage 30

Connecting People

Read: John 1:19–28

Hook: Looking back, who introduced you to a person who became significant in your life?

Book: Even though John the Baptist was misidentified with other important people, He clearly understood his role to introduce others to Jesus. He pushed the limelight away from himself to the Lord, *the thongs of whose sandals* John was *not worthy to untie*. He was simply a *voice calling in the desert* to point people home to God through faith in Jesus.

Took: Sadly, too many people fail to understand their need to be connected to the Savior. Who needs you to follow John's example by pointing them to Jesus? What could you do?

Passage 31

Barriers to God

Read: John 1:29–34

❖

Hook: What kind of barriers do people build between themselves and God?

Book: John cleared up any confusion about his role by pointing to Jesus as the *Lamb of God who takes away the sin of the world.* It had been revealed to John that Jesus would be the ultimate Sacrificial Lamb who would deal with sin once and for all (see Isaiah 53:12). The death of Jesus would remove the barrier of sin existing between God and man since the Garden of Eden. People can try what they may, but only Jesus has the ability to *take away* sin. That is why faith in Him is essential.

Took: What would change in your life if you really believed that the Lamb of God has taken away your sin?

Passage 32

It's Not About You

Read: John 1:35–39

Hook: Why are people so stuck on themselves?

Book: John gladly pointed his followers away from himself and toward Jesus. He was willing to fade into the background so that people could love and follow the One they really needed. John's glory came by giving it away.

Took: How does self-serving pride hinder you from helping people follow Jesus?

PASSAGE 33

No Fear

READ: JOHN 1:40–51

⁂

HOOK: Why do people often hesitate to share their religious or spiritual opinions?

BOOK: The first two followers of Jesus could not contain their excitement. They felt compelled to tell the people they loved about the Lord. Andrew immediately told his brother, Simon Peter, and *brought him to Jesus*. Philip went and shared the good news with his skeptical friend Nathanael. God used a simple invitation to change their lives. Is it a coincidence that the first two recorded examples of outreach involve family and friends?

TOOK: Who in your sphere of friendship needs to meet Jesus? How could you make the introduction?

PASSAGE 34

A Glimpse of Glory

READ: JOHN 2:1–12

HOOK: What elements do you think are essential to a true miracle?

BOOK: This first miracle revealed great things about Jesus. He must be from God since He can create, and He must be superior to their religious rituals that used the jars He borrowed. But, most of all, it *revealed His glory* to His followers so that they believed. Just seeing a simple flash of God's glory or ability should stimulate commitment to Him.

TOOK: Can you think of a time when you caught a glimpse of God's glory or ability in some situation? What kind of faith response was God seeking from you?

Passage 35

Upside-Down Worship

Read: John 2:13–22

Hook: What do you think God would like or dislike in worship practices today?

Book: In His first temple cleansing, Jesus repudiated the abuses of the greedy religious establishment. They were taking advantage of their temple positions so they could sell animals and exchange currency to pad their pockets at the expense of even the poor who could only afford doves. The Lord's drastic actions reminded them that worship is about God, not them, and that His followers must invest their efforts in helping, not hurting, others who worship the Lord.

Took: What could you do to make your church an inviting place for all kinds of people to know and worship the Lord?

PASSAGE 36

The Nature of Human Nature

READ: JOHN 2:23–25

HOOK: Which part of human nature disappoints you the most?

BOOK: Evidently, some of the people who witnessed the dramatic cleansing of the temple were prompted to confess faith in Jesus for selfish reasons. The omniscient Lord saw through these false believers and refused to trust Himself into their circle. Human nature can be so twisted by sin that it will even manipulate the goodness of God for selfish purposes.

TOOK: What can you do to protect yourself from the daily attacks of your own selfish human nature? How would you recognize genuine faith in yourself?

PASSAGE 37

Born Again

READ: JOHN 3:1–21

❖

HOOK: Which various paths do people follow to land themselves in heaven?

BOOK: According to Jesus, there is only one path to heaven: *Very truly I tell you, no one can see the kingdom of God unless he is born again.* He explained that His followers must have two births: a physical birth through their mothers, *water and flesh,* and a spiritual birth prompted by the *Spirit* through faith. So people of any age can enjoy a second birth, the spiritual birth, if they believe in him (verse 16). According to Jesus, this new birth is essential for heaven and provides salvation for the soul.

TOOK: If you are not sure that you have been born again, tell the Father that you believe in His son, Jesus, and ask Him to forgive your sins. Why is birth such an appropriate metaphor for becoming a follower of Jesus?

PASSAGE 38

Celebrating Others

READ: JOHN 3:22–36

HOOK: What hinders you from celebrating the successes of others?

BOOK: Since John had a realistic view of himself and of Jesus, he was able to publicly declare: *He must become greater; I must become less.* John knew that Jesus was God's Son, with all the abilities and knowledge John didn't have. For humbling himself and celebrating Jesus, John has been rewarded with honor through the centuries. He knew that the way up is down.

TOOK: After examining John's description of Jesus in this passage, in what ways do you think Jesus should play a greater role in your life?

PASSAGE 39

Crossing Racial Lines

READ: JOHN 4:1–26

HOOK: What thoughts, if any, do you experience when talking to a stranger who is racially or culturally different from you?

BOOK: Jesus crossed cultural, religious, and racial divides to talk with this woman and reveal Himself. He wanted all people, regardless of background, to enjoy *Living Water* to satisfy their thirst for God. By believing in Jesus as the Messiah, the woman would receive forgiveness from her life of sin and, in addition, gain freedom from false traditions. The message of Jesus was so liberating that He had unusual acceptance with people from different backgrounds.

TOOK: In the mosaic of society you interact daily with people from different backgrounds. How could they see acceptance in you so that the message of Christ can be heard?

PASSAGE 40

Hunger Pains

READ: JOHN 4:27–42

❧

HOOK: Can you think of an activity that you would skip a meal to do?

BOOK: Talking with this woman was better than food to Jesus for all the right reasons. Simply said, *"My food is to do the will of Him who sent me and to finish His work."* Every day Jesus looked for people like this woman, who were deceived by traditions, attitudes, or personal failures. Just as food nourishes the body, His passion for bringing people home to the Father satisfied the longing of His heart. When God's work becomes your daily food, the result is that people believe in Jesus as *the Savior of the world.*

TOOK: Try an experiment to develop your hunger for the right kind of food. Skip one meal this week and spend that time helping a person who is not a Jesus follower. Write out your plan and the results.

Ministry in Galilee

Passages 41–104

Passage 41

Need a Miracle?

Read: John 4:43–54

Hook: If you could receive a miracle from God today, what would be your request?

Book: Knowing that Jesus had turned water into wine, this anxious father realized that Jesus had the power to heal his son. He asked and got what he wanted, a miracle from God. All he had to do was simply take Jesus at His word. Unlike this father, not everyone gets a miracle exactly the way they hope—even Jesus had to suffer and die. But all can imitate His trust and obedience. Perhaps the real miracle God wants is to transform you as you learn to trust Him and His words fully.

Took: In the situation where you covet a miracle, how do you need to be more trusting that God will do what is right for you?

PASSAGE 42

Hometown Rejection

READ: LUKE 4:16–30

HOOK: Can you remember a time when you were surprised by a conflict with someone you had known most of your life?

BOOK: Jesus was not only rejected but almost killed by people in His hometown. They were excited about His miraculous abilities and His teaching until He applied the Scriptures to them. To justify themselves, they were even willing to destroy one of their own.

Even the people closest to you will resist spiritual truth. Since they think the message is for others and not for them, they attack the messenger who dares to try. *Jesus came to His own and His own received him not.* They wanted His glory but were not willing to submit to His message. His preaching exposed their jealousy, disobedience, and anger.

TOOK: Since familiarity can breed contempt, how could you prepare yourself for the day it comes your way?

PASSAGE 43

Closed Doors

READ: MATTHEW 4:13–17

HOOK: Can you think of a time when one door of opportunity closed in your life only to allow a better door to open? What emotions did you endure during the wait?

BOOK: After rejection in His hometown, Jesus moved to make Capernaum His center of ministry. As the quote from Isaiah predicted, the rejection in Nazareth allowed Him to take the message to the Gentiles in Galilee. When a door shuts, God opens another to fulfill His purposes. Sometimes the Father pushes people into fresh opportunities to help *people living in darkness see a great light.*

TOOK: When a door closes, how could you position yourself to see God's new opportunity?

Passage 44

Gone Fishing

Read: Luke 5:1–11, See also Matthew 4:18–22 and Mark 1:16–20

❖

Hook: Why do you think most people float through life as if they have no calling from God?

Book: Jesus took a stubborn fisherman and transformed him into an eager fisher of men. Once Peter was confronted with his personal sinfulness and granted grace, he was willing to leave everything to thrust himself into God's calling to reach others. Callings in life may differ, but there is a common thread that ties them together. Jesus wants everyone to help people they know come home to Him. Is there any commission on earth with greater value?

Took: What is a specific calling God has for your life? How should fishing for souls impact that role?

Passage 45

Authority Matters

Read: Mark 1:21–28, See also Luke 4:31–37

Hook: How can you tell when a leader has authority, not just a position?

Book: The people were amazed with the authority Jesus demonstrated in His teaching. Unlike other teachers, He had both firsthand knowledge and unique passion for God's truth, which set Him apart. He backed up His teaching by demonstrating His authority over demons. Jesus made quite a statement by making one of His first miracles the removal of a demon from a man in their house of worship. This symbolism foretold much of His future ministry on earth.

Took: Unlike many of the worshipers, the demon recognized Jesus. How would your life change if you truly honored the authority of Jesus?

Passage 46

Seeing Through Sickness

Read: Luke 4:38–41, See also Matthew 8:14–17 and Mark 1:29–34

Hook: When did you last sit alongside the bed of a sick person and wonder why this suffering was happening?

Book: Jesus demonstrated His authority to *rebuke the fever* and cast out demons. Every healing by Jesus is a reminder that sin and pain are not His plan and that He will ultimately do what is necessary to remove the curse that causes it. This snapshot of His healing mercies reminds you to look through your pain to enjoy the comfort and eventual victory of the Lord. He silenced the demons so that His path to the Cross and victory would not be interrupted prematurely.

Took: Even though you or a loved one may not receive a healing from Jesus, can you think of other ways you could *rebuke* the sickness and pain? What does Jesus desire for you to see beyond the suffering?

Passage 47

Good News Is for Sharing

Read: Luke 4:42–44, See also Matthew 4:23–25 and Mark 1:35–39

Hook: Describe a person in your circle of friends who might be clueless concerning the real person or message of Jesus.

Book: Unlike the people in Nazareth, who drove Jesus out of His hometown, these folks in Capernaum begged Him to stay. Jesus could easily have lingered to provide more teaching, but His passion for outreach pushed Him to leave in order to serve more people. Be careful not to allow people or circumstances to make you so comfortable that you fail to extend yourself to share God's good news with others. It is the one message everyone in the world must have.

Took: What overt or subtle pressures hinder you from sharing the message of Jesus with others? How should you deal with these pressures?

Passage 48

Jesus is Willing

Read: Luke 5:12–16, See also Matthew 8:2–4
and Mark 1:40–45

Hook: Why do you not always get what you request from the Lord?

Book: This man with leprosy got exactly what he asked for, healing. Leprosy was a death sentence, which symbolizes the spreading and life-destroying consequences of sin. This poor leper pictured for everyone the proper way to respond to God. He humbled himself, expressed his faith in Jesus, and followed with obedience. Humility releases the work of God in your life.

Took: What is Jesus willing to do in your life that you are not willing to humble yourself to do?

Passage 49

Connecting the Dots

Read: Luke 5:17–26, See also Matthew 9:1–8 and Mark 2:1–12

Hook: What key facts do people overlook when they doubt God's existence or ability?

Book: The healing ministry of Jesus attracted this throng of religious teachers and leaders from all over the country. Sadly, they could not make the connection that His miracles revealed His true identity as God, which gave Him the ability to forgive sin. After this healing, their doubts turned into amazement and praise. Thankfully, Jesus is patient to reveal Himself repeatedly so that people connect the dots and believe in Him.

Took: How can you help your friends connect the dots so that they stand in awe of Jesus too?

PASSAGE 50

Good Enough for God?

READ: LUKE 5:27, SEE ALSO MATTHEW 9:9–13 AND MARK 2:13–17

HOOK: Why do some people feel like they could never fully please God?

BOOK: Since Levi was despised as a first-century tax collector for the Romans, Jesus was criticized for selecting him as a disciple and for enjoying company with his associates. These religious leaders piously assumed that this group was unworthy and inferior. Jesus made it clear that true religion is not about the self-righteous but sinners. In their zeal to judge others, they simply revealed their own inferiority and need of a Savior. Anyone can be accepted by God if they accept His terms—repentance.

TOOK: What do you miss when you judge others? If you had a Levi banquet, what would it look like?

PASSAGE 51

Food Fight

READ: LUKE 5:33–39, SEE ALSO MATTHEW 9:14–17 AND MARK 2:18–22

HOOK: What was the craziest thing you ever did with food?

BOOK: How would you like to be a guest eating at Levi's banquet and have a religious leader confront you publicly about fasting? Awkward! This craziness about food only revealed the religious leaders' dependence on their layers of religious traditions, which Jesus rejected. They had so corrupted God's original teaching that Jesus compared their customs to an old wineskin that breaks when filled with God's truth. Manmade rules and traditions can easily become a substitute for obeying God's Word.

TOOK: Which contemporary traditions tend to blind people to themselves and the real message of the Bible?

Passage 52

Leap of Faith

Read: John 5:1–9

⁂

Hook: What do you think are some "leaps of faith" that people feel they must make to believe in Jesus?

Book: When Jesus met this man who had suffered for thirty-eight years, His compassion compelled Him to offer His best—Himself. The Lord's question—*Do you want to get well?*—was an invitation to the invalid to trust Jesus. Every issue in life, whether great or small, is a test of a person's faith in God and His ability. This man made the leap of a lifetime.

Took: Like the invalid, is there an area in your spiritual life where you are sitting and not walking? What leap of faith do you need to take?

PASSAGE 53

Calling Good "Bad"

READ: JOHN 5:10–18

HOOK: Can you recall a time when your good intentions were misunderstood?

BOOK: A chief characteristic of evil is that it calls good "bad." Immediately after Jesus miraculously healed this man, His actions were denounced for being done on the Sabbath. Duh! The religious leaders had created thirty-nine rules for Sabbath-keeping, and picking up a mat was not on the list of what was allowed. When Jesus explained that even the *Father is always at His work*, He made them even madder by *calling God His own Father, making Himself equal with God.* Their efforts to call Jesus' work "bad" merely opened a door to reveal His true goodness and greatness.

TOOK: Why do people call good "bad"? What suggestions would you have for a person who is misunderstood or criticized unjustly?

PASSAGE 54

Words Matter

READ: JOHN 5:19–30

HOOK: Which quote from a famous person do you use the most? Why?

BOOK: In the previous passage Jesus was condemned because His words equated Him with God the Father. In this answer, He revealed that He and the Father are so closely linked that *all judgment* has been placed in His hands. Even more, believing the words of Jesus is essential for eternal life (verses 24–27) since His words will be the basis for future judgment. What these religious leaders called blasphemy was in reality revelation and hope from God. The words of Jesus mattered then, matter today, and will matter forever.

TOOK: Since God's *just* judgment is based on the words of Jesus, how can you make His words matter even more in your life?

PASSAGE 55

Defending Yourself

READ: JOHN 5:31–47

❦

HOOK: How should you defend yourself when your character is attacked?

BOOK: In this passage, Jesus is still defending Himself for healing the invalid man on the Sabbath. He rejects the judgment of men and appeals to the grander testimonies about Him by John the Baptist, the Father, the Scriptures, and Moses. His critics would rather enjoy the *praise of each other* than these witnesses for Christ. Jesus knew that their rejection of Him included rejecting His witnesses as well. Even though His detractors thought they were complying with the writings of Moses, these same words would haunt and judge them one day. Jesus rested in the defense of His witnesses, not the expectations or demands of men.

TOOK: What does the example of Jesus teach you about defending yourself when unfairly attacked by others?

Passage 56

In Your Face

Read: Luke 6:1–11, See also Matthew12:1–14
and Mark 2:23–36

Hook: When was the last time you bumped into a rule that was insensitive to people?

Book: Jesus kept bumping into manmade rules for Sabbath keeping. After the religious establishment criticized His disciples for picking and eating grain, He put the issue in their faces by healing a man's hand right in their synagogue. Evidently it was permissible for them to criticize on the Sabbath but not for Jesus to heal. Not only did Jesus expose their hypocrisy, He revealed that He is the *Lord of the Sabbath* and He makes the rules. Jesus was always willing to confront those who controlled or hurt His people.

Took: Whom do you know who is suffering from a controlling person? What could be done to expose the hypocrisy of the situation?

PASSAGE 57

The Masses Get It

READ: MARK 3:7–12, SEE ALSO MATTHEW 12:15–21

HOOK: What issues cause a group to resist its leader?

BOOK: Even though the leaders refused to accept the teaching of Jesus, the people and even the demons got it. The people knew that their leaders were about control and power while Jesus was all righteousness and grace. Their enthusiasm was so great that a boat had to be prepared as a pulpit. For obvious reasons, this crowd chose to follow Jesus instead of their leaders.

TOOK: Who is looking to you for spiritual leadership? What can you learn from Jesus' model of leadership?

Passage 58

Prayer Prep

Read: Luke 6:12–16, See also Mark 3:13–19

Hook: Why do people tend to merely give lip service to prayer before making a major decision?

Book: Jesus spent the entire night in prayer before making one of His most critical choices, appointing His twelve apostles. These men would represent him during His life on earth and after He returned to the Father. He placed much of His life and ministry into their hands. If God's Son needed intense prayer like this, what does it say about your need?

Took: What did Jesus know about prayer that you may have forgotten? What major issue in your life needs serious "prep" time in prayer?

PASSAGE 59

Be Happy

READ: MATTHEW 5:1–12, SEE ALSO LUKE 6:17–26

HOOK: What things that you chase in life fail to deliver the happiness you expect?

BOOK: The famous Beatitudes of Jesus presented His approach to true happiness and fulfillment. In a religious world that stressed outward conformity to human traditions, He provided a breath of fresh air by calling people to real joy flowing from inner loyalty to God and His Word. The contrast was evident when the joy of Jesus was compared to the anger of the leaders. Jesus wanted people to know that anyone, anywhere, under any circumstances could look to God for joy by simply honoring His ways. Each of the Beatitudes reveals a way to express passion for God and the blessing that follows this passion.

TOOK: Which Beatitude captures your imagination the most? How do you want it to impact your life today?

Passage 60

Touch Your World

Read: Matthew 5:13–16

Hook: In your sphere of influence, who needs God in a big way? Why?

Book: Jesus used two metaphors to show His followers how anyone can make a difference in the lives of others. First, righteousness can preserve society just as *salt* preserved meat in ancient times. Making righteous choices can influence the moral standard in your circle of friends and family. Second, just as a lamp lights up a room, modeling and sharing God's truth will bring God's *light* to others. Cursing the darkness is easy, but think of the potential if every believer lighted a candle in the world. The Lord's dream is that people *may see your good deeds and praise your Father in heaven.* Your salt and light will make a difference beyond their size.

Took: What would need to change in your life to better spread some salt or light in your circle of influence?

Passage 61

Measure Yourself

Read: Matthew 5:17–20

Hook: Why do so many people feel like failures before God?

Book: The Sabbath controversies became a cause to question Jesus' regard for the Law of Moses. In this defense, He not only endorsed the Law but presented Himself as the fulfillment of both its prophecies and righteous standards. The real issue was much deeper. His conflict with the religious leadership stemmed from their failure to measure by the truth and spirit of the Law. They had more concern for knowledge and power than pleasing the God of heaven with submission. Since God's measurement in eternity will be based on obedience to His Word, that is the path to spiritual success for everyone.

Took: Overcoming feelings of failure is usually only an obedient step away. How would obedience in your life make you feel successful before God?

PASSAGE 62

Dartboard

READ: MATTHEW 5:21–26

HOOK: Whose picture is on the dartboard of your heart? Why do violent thoughts easily invade the mind?

BOOK: Jesus' words made people wonder if anyone could claim innocence from murder. Since murder flows from anger, He equated the two and warned people not to ignore the devastating results of unresolved anger. Jesus illustrated that anger can take forms like calling others names or harboring grudges. Whatever the form, the result is the same: broken relationships with people and with God.

TOOK: Is the cancer of anger eating away your joy? How can you remove that picture from your dartboard by moving toward reconciliation?

Passage 63

Lust Leftovers

Read: Matthew 5:27–32

Hook: How is sex a dominant factor in contemporary society, and what are the results?

Book: Society plays up lust, but not its outcome. Jesus warned that lust leads to adultery, which often results in divorce. Lust makes a selfish statement to your spouse that he or she is not good enough for you. Jesus used drastic language to warn against the consequences of lust. He knew that the games people play in their minds are not worth the painful results. Lust is a killer.

Took: How can you protect yourself from lust? How can you help others who have been hurt by the leftovers of lust?

Passage 64

Liar, Liar, Pants on Fire!

Read: Matthew 5:33–37

Hook: What are some creative ways you lead people to believe something that is not true?

Book: "Liar, liar, pants on fire!" goes the children's saying. That may be truer than you think (Revelation 21:8; 22:15). The first-century practice of taking an oath in such a way that it would not be binding was replaced by Jesus with simple truth-telling. Jesus took lying seriously since it violated the character of God—He is truth. Any deception beyond a simple "yes" or "no" comes from Satan. You can depend on God's truth, and others should be able to trust your words as well.

Took: How has bending the truth or lying become a part of your life? Why is lying so damaging to relationships? How would life change if you simply *let your "Yes" be "Yes" and your "No," be "No"*?

Passage 65

Sweet Revenge

Read: Matthew 5:38–42

⚜

Hook: Why is getting even with others overrated?

Book: Revenge may feel good, but it doesn't work. Just when you think you have won, you discover that you really lost. Jesus used some common-known laws of retaliation to show a better way. Instead of exacting everything due you from others, demonstrate humility and faith by turning the cheek, giving your coat, or walking the extra mile. Revenge doesn't satisfy, but trusting yourself to God's eventual justice and care does.

Took: Why would someone be shocked if you granted generosity instead of revenge? Who needs you to turn the other cheek or walk an extra mile?

Passage 66

Loving Your Enemies

Read: Matthew 5:43–48, See also Luke 6:27–36

❖

Hook: Who are the hardest people in your world for you to love?

Book: How would you like to look in the mirror and see a reflection of your Heavenly Father? Jesus said that one of the best ways to show you are God's child is to *love your enemies.* That unique trait makes you more like God than anything else. In fact, Jesus identified it with perfection.

Took: Why is loving people who have hurt you contrary to human nature? What boundaries did Jesus model in loving people? Who needs undeserved grace from you?

PASSAGE 67

Money Motives

READ: MATTHEW 6:1–4

HOOK: What motivates people to make financial donations to charity?

BOOK: Some people give to get, but what they receive pales in comparison to what they could have had. How could the temporary applause of people ever compare to the eternal reward of God? When you give to the needy to impress people instead of God, you make a statement about your heart. Jesus is not asking for secrecy but for pure motives. He must be pleased when the poor in spirit bless the poor in means.

TOOK: Since anonymous giving purifies motives, who could you surprise with a random act of kindness? Be generous and secret. How do you think they will feel?

PASSAGE 68

Fear of Praying

READ: MATTHEW 6:5–8

HOOK: Why do some people fear praying aloud in front of others?

BOOK: Possibly this fear stems from pressures and abuses they see in the praying styles of other people. Jesus rebuked hypocrites who made praying a sport hoping to be seen by others. These people often view others as inferior. Since Jesus said that *your Father knows what you need before you ask Him*, prayer does not require eloquence but dependence. Instead of being a prideful act, it should stimulate humble trust and hope in God. Remember, prayer has an audience of One.

TOOK: How does this passage strengthen your prayer life? Even though prayer is for God, who would be encouraged to hear you pray out loud?

Passage 69

Living the Lord's Prayer

Read: Matthew 6:9–15

Hook: Why do people get distracted or bored during prayer?

Book: Could it be that many don't know how to pray God's way? Jesus taught His followers this prayer, which contains six petitions. The first three contain reminders about God and His Kingdom, and the final three reflect how to live. When prayers begin by praising God, it logically flows into a desire to trust Him. But wait! Jesus followed this prayer with more exhortation on forgiveness in verses 14 and 15. Could it be that the ultimate test of your prayer life is to get off your knees to extend forgiveness? Praying God's way will make you more forgiving, like He is.

Took: How does each petition in the Lord's Prayer draw you closer to the Father? Do you see a connection between forgiveness and each petition?

Passage 70

Full from Fasting

Read: Matthew 6:16–18

Hook: Why do you think fasting has become somewhat of a lost art?

Book: Jesus had some great news about fasting. It is not about food or other people but about God. People went to extreme measures to broadcast their eating sacrifices just to impress others. They missed some great food for nothing. Like giving and prayer, fasting was an act of sacrifice intended to honor the Father. The time saved can be used in personal worship. The rewards for fasting are greater than a smaller waistline or momentary praise because they will come from the Father Himself. You can eat and drink to that!

Took: Skip a meal or two this week and spend the time with the Heavenly Father instead. What do you think you will discover?

PASSAGE 71

It's Only Money, Honey

READ: MATTHEW 6:19–24

HOOK: How would you respond to this quote: "The more you own, the more it owns you"?

BOOK: It is easy to see that earthly treasures can be stolen or rust away, but the real dangers are more subtle. Jesus warned His followers that treasures can blind them and bring spiritual darkness to their souls. The result is that people may choose money as master rather than God.

TOOK: What is the real cost of failing to honor God with your money? How does generous giving liberate a believer?

Passage 72

Worry-Free Living

Read: Matthey 6:25–34

Hook: Why is worry such a big part of life in today's world?

Book: Don't you wish there was a pill for worry? Even though stopping seems impossible, Jesus provided an antidote. He said to replace worry with confident faith in the Heavenly Father. If your happiness is controlled by food, drink, your body, or clothes, of course you will worry. But, when you actively choose God and His righteousness, you will receive all these things and so much more. Worry discounts faith.

Took: What is at the top of your worry list? How does this passage put that worry into perspective?

PASSAGE 73

What Is in Your Eye?

READ: MATTHEY 7:1–6, SEE ALSO LUKE 6:37–42

HOOK: When was the last time someone misjudged you?

BOOK: Just imagine what walking around with a plank protruding from your eye would do to your relationships—bump! This self-righteous lifestyle damages objectivity to you, others, and even your antagonists (*dogs* and *pigs*). Jesus wants you to know that your measurement for others will haunt you and reveal more than you wish. Only the person who deals with his own plank is ever qualified to gently remove any speck from a friend's eye.

TOOK: Why is being judged so hurtful? What precautions should be taken when helping someone remove a speck from his eye?

PASSAGE 74

Behind the Door

READ: MATTHEW 7:7–12

HOOK: How would you describe the expectation level of people when they pray?

BOOK: Jesus wants you to know there is a Heavenly Father behind the door who hears and cares about your prayers and will respond to persistent dependence on Him. You can be assured He will answer only with *good gifts*. You can imitate the Father's generosity in prayer by practicing the Golden Rule. After all, that is how He treats others. Living according to God's Word will bring the answer to many prayers.

TOOK: How could practicing the Golden Rule be the answer to someone's prayer today?

PASSAGE 75

The Minority View

READ: MATTHEW 7:13–14

HOOK: How do followers of Jesus sometimes feel different from people who don't believe?

BOOK: Jesus explained the difference with this metaphor. The few who choose to believe in Him enter the small gate that leads to the narrow path that results in life. Unfortunately, the majority are unbelievers who enter the wide gate that leads to a broad road that ends in destruction. Since Jesus is the small gate, faith in Him makes all the difference. Are you in the minority or majority?

TOOK: In the Sermon on the Mount (Matthew chapters 5 through 7), Jesus championed a unique lifestyle for His followers. How would you describe the distinctiveness the Lord expects of believers?

Passage 76

A Scary Passage

Read: Matthew 7:15–23, See also Luke 6:43–45

⚜

Hook: What are various opinions on getting a ticket into heaven? Who makes the rules?

Book: Scary passage! The religious leaders thought they had a lock on heaven because of their knowledge, position, or works. Jesus made it clear that heaven is all about something these guys didn't have, obedience—but only those *who do the will of My Father who is in heaven* will enter it. The will of the Father is to believe in His Son and obey His words. These leaders should have been more concerned about the applause of heaven than of men. The passage ends with a brutal evaluation: God doesn't even know them, and what they think is good He calls evil. Genuine inner faith is demonstrated in external obedience.

Took: How would doing the *will of the Father* remove your fears and embolden your personal walk with God?

PASSAGE 77

Weathering Storms

READ: MATTHEW 7:24–29, SEE ALSO LUKE 6:46–49

HOOK: What approaches do people use to cope with the storms of life?

BOOK: Jesus wants His followers to know that His words provide the wisdom and strength to weather the difficulties of life. They need to build the structure of their lives on a biblical foundation.

Unlike the teachers of the day who merely quoted others or sounded hollow, Jesus came across with authority because He revealed God's truth when addressing real human needs and questions. Lives built on His words can handle all the challenges of life.

TOOK: How could you develop your inner strength from God's Word to be prepared for the storms of life?

Passage 78

Standing Out

READ: LUKE 7:1–10, SEE ALSO MATTHEW 8:5–13

HOOK: Can you describe a person whose Christian faith amazed you?

BOOK: Since when does a commanding Roman centurion humble himself before a roaming Jewish preacher? Unlike the nation of Israel, this Gentile recognized the authority and power of Jesus. Even the Lord was amazed: *"I tell you, I have not found such great faith even in Israel."* This centurion was an example of the faith and obedience Jesus deserved. His humble faith in Christ made him stand out in an arrogant and selfish culture. He got what he wanted and more.

TOOK: Which situation in your life would permit you to startle others with a bold trust in the Lord?

PASSAGE 79

Bumping into Strangers

READ: LUKE 7:11–17

HOOK: When was the last time you were surprised by the unexpected kindness of a stranger?

BOOK: When compassion flows in you, it will spill over and touch others. Jesus could not contain Himself when He saw the desperate situation of this widow. He had to act. Much of His ministry recorded in the Bible took place as Jesus simply interacted with people in His travels. Can you imagine how grateful that widow was to bump into a stranger who cared enough to help her?

TOOK: How could you be more alert to the needs of the of the people God places in your path each day?

Passage 80

Honest Questions

Read: Luke 7:18–35, See also Matthew 11:1–11

Hook: Why do you think some faithful believers in Jesus may harbor questions about faith?

Book: Since John the Baptist was in prison and could not personally observe the ministry of Jesus, he sent his followers to ask questions. Jesus simply replied that His work testified to His identity as Messiah. John's question must have been from a pure heart because Jesus went beyond His answer to praise John as above all others. He and John shared a common message but had different styles. God welcomes honest questions because they open the door to transforming answers.

Took: What fears do you have when people ask you faith questions? How could you help them balance their questions with faith?

Passage 81

Is God Fair?

Read: Matthew 11:20–24

Hook: What issues do people raise that question the fairness of God?

Book: This passage reveals that God's work and judgment must be viewed in light of His comprehensive knowledge. In denouncing the cities that did not believe, Jesus revealed insight into God's judgment. First, judgment is based on the amount of revelation provided to people. Second, God knew the potential responses of the other cities if they had been presented with the miracles. Third, judgment always reflects the people's response. What finite minds wrestle with is very clear to God. His ways and judgments can be fully trusted.

Took: Why do people question the integrity or fairness of God? Why is God the appropriate Person to nuance judgment and rewards?

Passage 82

God's Inner Circle

Read: Matthew 11:25–30

Hook: What kind of religious people or situations make you feel excluded?

Book: Jesus invited people to lay aside the traditions and burdens of their religious system and come to Him for rest. Those who considered themselves *wise and learned* arrogantly rejected Jesus and His followers. In contrast, people could come to Jesus like *little children* by simply believing the truths He revealed. Instead of heavy rules, they would find the *yoke* of Jesus easy and light. It is refreshing to discover that simple obedience yokes you with the God of heaven.

Took: Which religious traditions seem burdensome to you? How does being yoked to Jesus bring freedom and empowerment?

Passage 83

Confession Is Good for the Soul

Read: Luke 7:36–50

Hook: Why does judging others come so naturally?

Book: Jesus used the thankful heart of this sinful woman to expose the hard heart of this religious leader. She was brutally honest about her sin and need of forgiveness, while Simon winked at His own failures. By comparing himself to her, Simon felt justified. Jesus wanted him to know that love is the natural response to God's gracious forgiveness. Simon's lack of love revealed an unforgiving heart that failed to see the depths of his own sin. It was easier to recognize her sin than to admit his own. The woman's confession brought her salvation and peace.

Took: Why is it so difficult to acknowledge sin? Who would experience more love if you did some confessing?

PASSAGE 84

The Unpardonable Sin

READ: MATTHEW 12:22–37, SEE ALSO MARK 3:20–30

⁂

HOOK: Why do people struggle with feeling totally forgiven by God?

BOOK: When Jesus healed this man, the people properly deduced that He was Messiah, *Son of David*. Immediately, the religious leaders reacted and committed the sin that cannot be forgiven. They blatantly rejected the miracles and deity of Jesus, claiming they were done by the power of Satan instead of by the Holy Spirit. Their words revealed their lack of faith in Jesus and would be used against them in the Judgment. They actually condemned themselves by refusing to believe. Every sin is forgivable except the blasphemy of unbelief. Think how different the Jesus story would be if they had believed.

TOOK: When did you believe in Jesus as your Savior and Lord? How does God's forgiveness motivate you?

Passage 85

Stubborn Rejecters

Read: Matthew 12:38–45

✤

Hook: How would you describe a contrary personality? Why do some people like to take this stance?

Book: Some people refused to understand. In the previous passage, the religious leaders brazenly condemned Jesus for healing a blind and mute man. Now, they requested another miracle. Jesus had had enough. He addressed them as a *wicked and adulterous generation* and refused another sign until His resurrection, which would seal their doom. In the Judgment, their unbelief will so frustrate the *people of Nineveh* and the *Queen of the South* who believed, that they will condemn them as well. Even Jesus, the perfect One, had people reject Him.

Took: How do you think their rejection made Jesus feel? What makes people so stubbornly refuse to submit to Jesus?

PASSAGE 86

The Relationship Test

READ: MATTHEW 12:46–50, SEE ALSO MARK 3:31–35 AND LUKE 8:19–21

HOOK: What would cause you to doubt the genuineness of a person's faith in God?

BOOK: Jesus used the visit of His blood relatives to make a dramatic point about faith. Neither the family ties of His relatives or the steeped traditions of His audience were true indicators of a relationship with God. Genuine faith demonstrates itself by doing *the will of the Father in heaven*. The test of genuine faith is obedience to God's will as revealed in His teaching. Jesus knows believers won't be perfect but still considers them related to Him.

TOOK: Why does obedience connect you closer to the Savior? What strains exist in your relationship that obedience will heal for you?

Passage 87

Your Spiritual Garden

Read: Matthew 13:1–23, See also Mark 4:1–25
and Luke 8:1–18

Hook: What influences people so that they respond to God differently?

Book: With these parables, Jesus turns from His critics to reveal spiritual secrets to His followers. These four soils reflect four heart conditions. The hard *path* gives Satan opportunity; the *rocky places* cave to external pressures; the *thorns* choke faith with inner worry about life and possessions; but only the *good soil* receives the seed of God's Word and bears fruit at various levels. The way you control your heart attitude significantly affects how you respond to God's teaching. The spiritual fruit produced in your life indicates the condition of your heart's soil.

Took: What is required for you to maintain *good soil*, a heart receptive to God's Word?

Passage 88

A Lifelong Process

Read: Mark 4:26–29

Hook: How do people tend to be impatient with life or even with God?

Book: Instant gratification is not what it is purported to be. Jesus used the metaphor of the growing process that transforms a seed into a fruitful stalk of wheat to illustrate how the kingdom of God will develop and grow until Christ returns. Many of His followers impatiently wanted to see it all happen immediately. But Jesus, knowing the future, wanted them to understand that a process had to occur that would result in a *harvest*. You would be wise not to second-guess God's timing.

Took: How do you see the hand of God processing and maturing your walk with Him as your life progresses?

Passage 89

Fake Believers

Read: Matthew 13:24–30, 36–43

Hook: When were you disappointed as a person revealed his or her true character?

Book: Jesus warned His followers that everyone who claims to believe may not ring true. In the growing process, weeds can look similar to wheat until harvest time, when they are revealed to be fruitless. Satan has planted unbelievers among believers to hurt the harvest. Producing spiritual fruit in your life is critical to Jesus since it reveals your heart of faith and eternal destiny. Fruit is the standard by which you should evaluate yourself and others.

Took: How are you fooled by the lack of spiritual fruit in others? What fruit is Jesus looking for in your life?

Passage 90

Big Things Come in Small Packages

Read: Matthew 13:31–32, See also Mark 4:30–32

Hook: How would you like to see Christianity make a larger impact in the world?

Book: Jesus knew His followers must have felt insignificant in light of their small numbers and the fierce opposition coming their way. He reassured them with the parable of the mustard seed. Even though His Kingdom appeared too tiny to make a difference, it would grow and become a large resting place for many people. Never underestimate the power and growth of God's Kingdom. As you do Kingdom work, you will be surprised by who comes to perch on His branches.

Took: Since God's Kingdom will succeed, what could you be doing to help it grow into a resting place for many people?

Passage 91

A Cure for Discouragement

Read: Matthew 13:33–35, See also Mark 4:33–34

⁂

Hook: What common pressures discourage believers?

Book: Jesus knew that future events could easily dishearten His followers. The constant clamor of the opposition accompanied by His eventual death could wear them down with feelings of hopelessness. They needed to know that His Kingdom of righteousness and truth was like a small amount of yeast that would affect everything it touches. Just as the prophets predicted, the teachings of Jesus are true. No matter how difficult life appears, never underestimate the influence and ultimate victory of His message.

Took: How could your righteous choices release some yeast to bring hope to people you know?

Passage 92

Valuing the Right Stuff

Read: Matthew 13:44–46

Hook: Which personal possession do you prize the most?

Book: Like this man who found a treasure in a field and desired it so much that He bought the field, or like the merchant who found the fine pearls, Jesus wanted His followers to realize the true worth of serving in His Kingdom. Nothing is more valuable than possessing His truth and righteousness. This man discovered the joy He craved by simply selling the stuff that didn't count to get what did. No sacrifice compares with the treasure Jesus gives.

Took: Why is it so hard to give up your treasures to gain God's? Which possession hinders you the most? How would your life change if you *sold all* you *had and bought that field*?

PASSAGE 93

Equal Justice

READ: MATTHEW 13:47–50

⚜

HOOK: Why is it so easy to believe that God's justice is for others but not for you?

BOOK: Jesus wanted people to know that His Kingdom is open to all *fish* in the sea and His basis for judgment is identical for everyone. All bias or bigotry will dissolve when you face the Judge of heaven and earth. God is no respecter of persons and His judgment is sure. Like Jesus said: "Do you really understand *all these things*?"

TOOK: How do you tend to ignore God's judgment? How would you adjust your life if you really understood this teaching of Jesus?

PASSAGE 94

Open to New Ideas

READ: MATTHEW 13:51–53

⁂

HOOK: Why do people tend to be skeptical of new ideas? What results from this skepticism?

BOOK: Some people could not accept the teaching of Jesus because they mistakenly assumed that it contradicted the Old Testament. Jesus commended teachers who accepted and taught the wonderful unity of God's progressive revelation, which sees Jesus and His teaching connecting perfectly with the old. These people discovered that the things predicted by the prophets of old were fulfilled in Jesus. No wonder the apostle Paul stated in 2 Timothy 3:16 that *all Scripture is God-breathed and useful.*

TOOK: What pressures bind your thinking and stifle your walk with God? Can you think of issues where you read your opinions into the Bible?

Passage 95

Power Words

Read: Mark 4:35–41, See also Matthew 8:18, 23–27 and Luke 8:22–25

Hook: What do children mean when they say "Who says?" Why does this make a difference?

Book: After proclaiming His deity and message through parables, Jesus followed with this miracle to demonstrate His authority to say these things. Amazingly, all it took was His spoken word to both teach the parables and to still the storm. His words are powerful. The truthfulness and authority of words usually depends on the person speaking. Jesus left no doubt as how to deal with His.

Took: If *even the wind and the waves obey him*, what does that imply for you? What power is missing in your life because of failure to obey His teaching?

PASSAGE 96

Pig–itis

READ: MARK 5:1–20, SEE ALSO MATTHEW 8:28–34 AND LUKE 8:26–39

❖

HOOK: What is the most blatant display of selfishness you have witnessed recently?

BOOK: The term "pig" is often used to describe a person who only cares for himself at the expense of others. This demon-possessed man was extremely self-centered before his healing, but his dysfunction paled in comparison to the selfishness of the people. They were more concerned about their pigs than about his healing or the benevolent Jesus. Their greed and self-interest revealed a lack of love for people and lack of respect for God. What prevents you from celebrating a person's turnaround or rejoicing at God's grace to others?

TOOK: How do you think this man was accepted by the people after Jesus left? How does pig–itis reveal itself in relationships today?

Passage 97

Take a Knee

Read: Mark 5:21–43, See also Matthew 9:18–26 and Luke 8:40–56

Hook: Why is it so difficult to submit to others?

Book: Both Jairus and the sick woman bowed down on the ground before Jesus. One asked a favor and the other thanked him for one. In that atmosphere of rejection, their faith must have been refreshing to Jesus. Their humility was catalytic, enabling them to receive more than they dreamed. True humility flows from a realization of who Jesus is and a personal trust in Him. The better you know Him the more you will want to bend the knee in submission.

Took: What prevents you from trusting Jesus in the same way as these two did? In which area of your life is Jesus waiting for you to bend the knee?

PASSAGE 98

Blind Faith

READ: MATTHEW 9:27–34

HOOK: What has impressed you about blind people you have met?

BOOK: It has been said that blind people can often see better than those with sight. These two blind men proved that with their faith. Unlike the Pharisees, who refused to believe the miracles they could actually verify, these two had faith even when they could not see. The blind men could even recognize that Jesus was Messiah, *Son of David*. Some people think that believing in Jesus takes blind faith when in reality the facts are so obvious that even the blind can see them. Could it be that people with a greater understanding of their personal need are more open to faith? These leaders were blinded by their pride.

TOOK: What blind spots has pride created in your spiritual walk? How could your simple obedience help open the eyes of those you love?

PASSAGE 99

Hometown Jealousy

READ: MARK 6:1–6, SEE ALSO MATTHEW 13:54–58

HOOK: How have you been hurt by people who saw you grow up?

BOOK: The people in Jesus' hometown *took offense at Him* simply because He had wisdom and abilities they did not. Their inability to get past their familiarity and petty jealousies prevented them from believing in His divine person, which was confirmed by His teaching and miracles. The result was that they suffered since their lack of faith limited the miracles and healings in their community. It is tempting to think that you can be successful simply by despising those who are.

TOOK: Why does familiarity breed contempt? How should you respond when hurt by the jealousy of people you know or love?

Passage 100

The Compassionate Few

Read: Matthew 9:35–38, See also Mark 6:6

⚜

Hook: What would you list as the hallmarks of a compassionate person?

Book: Even though Jesus was rejected in His hometown, He was swarmed by others wherever He went. *When He saw the crowds, He had compassion on them because they were harassed and helpless, like sheep without a shepherd.* Since their spiritual leaders were consumed with power and personal gain, the people were drawn to the loving leadership of Jesus. Jesus invited His disciples to join Him by being *workers in His harvest field*. Even though they were *few*, God would answer their prayers, making them spiritual shepherds to the needy. A loving person attracts others and makes a difference in their lives.

Took: Why is it so easy to be part of the unloving majority? What would need to change in you to be mobilized to be one of the compassionate few?

Passage 101

Confidence in You

Read: Matthew 10:1–42, See also Mark 6:7–11 and Luke 9:1–5

❖

Hook: Why do people tend to feel inadequate to help others spiritually?

Book: Sending out the twelve disciples enabled Jesus to both multiply His ministry and provide experience to the disciples before He had to leave them. Notice that His charge was personal and full of specific information on what to do or not do. He warned them that they would share in the hostility that came His way and encouraged them to make the sacrifices necessary to be faithful. He wanted them to know that anyone who reached out to others in His name would *certainly not lose his reward*. Jesus not only has confidence in His followers but provides all the resources they need.

Took: If serving Jesus were easy, everyone would do it. Which instructions in this passage make you feel more confident in reaching out to others? Why does the reward overshadow the sacrifice?

Passage 102

A Lost Art

READ: MARK 6:12–13, SEE ALSO MATTHEW 11:1 AND LUKE 9:6

⚜

HOOK: Why do you think the word *repent* has been dropped from society's vocabulary?

BOOK: This brief passage records the core message and ministry of the twelve disciples Jesus sent out. They simply preached *repentance*—turning from disobedience and sin to faith in Jesus. The message was confirmed to their audiences by the power of Christ displayed in their ministry. Jesus often reminded people that they could not serve two masters. Devotion to the Creator and Savior demands a big turn from whatever enslaves a person back to the Lord. Believing seems easy, but repentance is another matter!

TOOK: Why are people often so callous to repentance? How could your life paint a picture of repentance for others to see?

Passage 103

Compliment of Compliments

Read: Mark 6:14–16, see also Matthew 14:1–2 and Luke 9:7–9

Hook: What is a high compliment you would like to receive during your life on earth?

Book: In the clamor of Jesus' popularity, King Herod Antipas tried to figure out His true identity. Realizing Jesus must be someone special, Herod only considered powerful people who were dead—a raised John the Baptist, Elijah, or an ancient prophet. He even contradicted current logic and exclaimed, *John, whom I beheaded, has been raised from the dead.* There could be no higher compliment for John the Baptist than to be confused with Jesus. When Herod witnessed the person and power of Jesus, he could only think of John.

Took: What does it require to become like Christ? How would you like for people to confuse you with Jesus?

Passage 104

Unfair People

Read: Mark 6:17–29, See also Matthew 14:3–12

Hook: Which unfair situation in your life lingers the most in your mind? How would you characterize an unfair person?

Book: Who says life is fair? John's earthly reward for fulfilling God's call was not pretty, but rather brutal and unfair. Anger has few boundaries and can become quite personal, defying logic. Not only did John have some loyal friends to care for his body, he was given the opportunity to go to heaven to be there when Jesus arrived. How do you think the two may have compared notes?

Took: After reading this passage, what advice would you give to a person enduring an unfairness that may result from living for the Lord?

Training the Disciples Around Galilee

Passages 105–133

Passage 105

Being Available

Read: Mark 6:30–34, See also Matthew 14:13–14, Luke 9:10–11 and John 6:1–3

Hook: What do you think are some common spiritual needs of people you know?

Book: When the twelve disciples returned from spreading the message Jesus had given them, they could hardly wait to tell their stories. Jesus wanted to take them off to a quiet place to reflect, but the needs of the people longing to hear Him grabbed His attention. The people knew Jesus had something they needed. *He had compassion on them, because they were like sheep without a shepherd.* Jesus interrupted what He wanted to do to take time to *teach them many things*. Their spiritual need overwhelmed Him and became His immediate priority.

Took: Who needs you to shepherd them spiritually? How could you position yourself to be more available to people in need?

Passage 106

What Is in Your Hands?

Read: Mark 6:35–44, See also Matthew 14:15–21, Luke 9:12–17, and John 6:4–13

Hook: How do people tend to grab credit that really belongs to God?

Book: A little success can go to your head. When the Twelve returned from their successful ministry ventures, Jesus used this miracle to remind them that their ability and success come only from God's grace and power. The Lord is able to take humble people and things, like loaves and fish, to reveal His glory and meet the needs of others. The Twelve had in their hands what they needed to feed the people; what they lacked was God's power. If you think ministry depends on your ability, you will merely fail. Service for God begins and ends with dependence on Him.

Took: What has God placed in your hands to help others? How could you demonstrate your dependence on God to others?

Passage 107

Selfish Desires

Read: John 6:14–15, See also Matthew 14:22–23 and Mark 6:45–46

Hook: What does it say about people that they are so anxious to get something for free?

Book: The feeding of the five thousand so impressed the masses that they wanted to make Jesus their king. He withdrew, knowing that what they truly desired was food and security instead of His teaching and mission. It is easy to desire or serve God for all the wrong reasons.

Took: Pride is insidious. How do selfish motivations warp your view of God and affect your involvement in spiritual activities?

Passage 108

Hard Hearts

READ: MARK 6:47–52, SEE ALSO MATTHEW 14:24–33
AND JOHN 6:16–21

HOOK: What makes it difficult for people to recognize the true identity of Jesus?

BOOK: The reason Jesus walked on water was to reveal His divinity to His disciples, who still failed to fully understand. *Their hearts were hardened* even after seeing the feeding of the five thousand. The beauty of Jesus was not His ability to perform miracles but the quality of His person as the Son of God. Fascination with what Jesus can do may overshadow respect for who He is. Everything He does flows from who He is.

TOOK: How might you insult God by wanting what He offers without respecting who He is? What should respect for His divinity look like in your life?

Passage 109

Hurting Hearts

Read: Mark 6:53–56, See also Matthew 14:34–36

Hook: Why do you think pain has been called God's megaphone?

Book: During His journey on earth, Jesus experienced two extremes—rejection and acceptance. The pain and sickness of these people created a passion that could only be satisfied by seeking a touch from Jesus. Personal hurts opened their hearts to the Lord and created a sense of urgency. When people suffer, they desire a person more than answers.

Took: What are some typical responses toward God when you suffer? How could you let disappointment or pain draw you closer to the Lord?

Passage 110

Essential Bread

Read: John 6:22–59

❦

Hook: Why do you think a simple piece of bread is so satisfying?

Book: Jesus loved metaphors and used bread to illustrate Himself. Believing in Jesus is compared to eating the *Bread of Life*. The only work that God requires is *to believe in the one He has sent*. As you read the passage, you will discover that the *Bread of Life* gives eternal life, satisfies, is available to all, reveals the Father, and so much more. Enjoying this bread is conditional on believing that Jesus is *the living bread that came down from heaven*. Do you believe in Him?

Took: Why is the metaphor of bread so appropriate to Jesus? How could your daily diet include more *Bread of Life*? Eat well!

Passage 111

Dangers of Criticism

Read: John 6:60–71

Hook: Why do people criticize something they don't understand? What does your criticism communicate about you?

Book: Since the disciples did not fully understand or appreciate the previous discourse of Jesus as the Bread of Life, they *grumbled*. Possibly, the reference to Judas indicates that he was the instigator of the criticism. There is one in every crowd. The result is that some of Christ's followers *turned back and no longer followed Him*. Sadly, the critical comments of a few had a dramatic influence on the spiritual state of others. Placing yourself above the words of Jesus is dangerous to both you and those listening.

Took: How have you seen critical people hurt the innocent? When confused about God or His Word, what are some healthy ways to seek understanding that would not be hurtful to others?

Passage 112

Substitute Rules

Read: Mark 7:1–23, See also Matthew 15:1–20 and John 7:1

❖

Hook: What is the silliest religious rule or tradition you have ever heard?

Book: Jesus discovered that people can have clean hands while tolerating a dirty heart. These critics valued washing their hands more than even honoring their parents, much less accepting the words of Jesus. Creating external rules can blind you to inner hypocrisy. Jesus let them know that *nothing outside a man can make him "unclean."* In fact, their silly rules and lack of faith in Him revealed their unclean hearts.

Took: Which traditions or activities in your life allow you to justify unclean behavior? What traditions could reveal that you have a clean heart?

PASSAGE 113

Unexpected Friendship

READ: MARK 7:24–30, SEE ALSO MATTHEW 15:21–28

HOOK: Can you remember a person who unexpectedly dropped into your life and brought you great joy?

BOOK: While being rejected by His own people, Jesus was trusted by this outsider. He played a little tough by explaining to this Gentile woman that He came first to feed the *children* (Israel). She responded by begging bread for the *dogs* (Gentiles). This is a snapshot of future events after the final rejection of Jesus when the good news would spread to the Gentile world. It also reminds you to watch for people whom God drops in your life who need His grace.

TOOK: How could you be on the alert for people God places in your path? What do you have that can bless them?

PASSAGE 114

Use and Abuse

READ: MARK 7:31–37, SEE ALSO MATTHEW 15:29–31

✣

HOOK: When was the last time you felt taken advantage of by a friend?

BOOK: These people begged for a miracle and got it. They were even *overwhelmed with amazement* by what Jesus did, but that is as far as it went. There is no confession to His person or faith that obeys. They were satisfied to use and abuse what Jesus offered. No wonder the masses would one day turn on Him.

TOOK: How do you think people use Jesus today instead of submitting in true trust and obedience? Can you think of ways you may abuse Him?

PASSAGE 115

Why Worry?

READ: MARK 8:1–9, SEE ALSO MATTHEW 15:32–38

HOOK: What are some of the ways you doubt God's ability?

BOOK: Why do you think Jesus fed these four-thousand-plus people like He did the five thousand as recorded two chapters earlier in the Gospel of Mark? Since this is a Gentile setting, was He demonstrating that His bread is for everyone? Was He giving His disciples and others a second chance to respond properly? People were *satisfied*, and there was an abundance left over. Jesus can be trusted to fully meet your needs. In fact, His ability overflows.

TOOK: What kind of statement does your worry make to God? What is your present challenge, and how should you trust Him fully?

Passage 116

Never Satisfied

Read: Matthew 15:39–16:4, See also Mark 8:9–12

Hook: Why do some people act as if they are never satisfied with your efforts?

Book: The religious establishment had too much at stake to accept Jesus. To bide for time, they repeatedly asked for signs of Messiah even though Jesus had already filled their eyes with miracles and their ears with truth proving His divinity. Their lack of satisfaction merely revealed that they were *a wicked and adulterous generation*. When Jesus would finally grant their wish for a sign, it would be His death and resurrection, which would seal their doom.

Took: What hidden motives cause people to reject Jesus? How could you demonstrate to others your total satisfaction with Him?

PASSAGE 117

Discernment

READ: MATTHEW 16:5–12, SEE ALSO MARK 8:13–21

HOOK: Why is yeast a good metaphor for false teaching? How have you ever been fooled by untrue information?

BOOK: The disciples demonstrated their innocence by not understanding Jesus' comments about bread and by their need to be warned about the false teaching of the Pharisees and Sadducees. The powerful position of the religious leaders was never to be confused with the "truth" of their teaching. Jesus knew that people need help discerning truth from error. False teaching is usually exposed by what a person says about Jesus and His Word.

TOOK: How can believers help each other be more discerning?

PASSAGE 118

Always Learning

READ: MARK 8:22–26

HOOK: What metaphor would you use to describe the path your spiritual life has taken?

BOOK: The oddity of this healing suggests that Jesus had something more in mind. Could it be that the stages in His healing of this man were meant to be a metaphor for the constant need of growth in the disciples' lives? There is always a next step or a new discovery as you walk with God.

TOOK: How has your spiritual life become stale? What is the next level of commitment God would desire for you?

Passage 119

Cracking a Tough Nut

Read: Matthew 16:13–20, See also Mark 8:27–30 and Luke 9:18–21

Hook: Who in your world is so far from God that you are tempted to give up on this person?

Book: In the midst of rejection, Jesus took the disciples to the side of a rocky mountain and heard the confession He had longed for: *You are the Messiah, the Son of the living God*. In spite of his previous ups and downs, Peter got it right this time. How did he understand so clearly? Jesus explained *that this was not revealed by flesh and blood, but by His Father in heaven*. The God who opened Peter's heart would also use him to serve people. God can crack the toughest nut!

Took: Jot down the names of a couple of tough nuts you know, and pray daily for the Father to reveal the truth to them. How could God use you to help soften their hearts?

Passage 120

Faith Questions

Read: Matthew 16:21–23, See also Mark 8:31–33 and Luke 9:22

⸙

Hook: Which questions about faith or God do you struggle with the most?

Book: When Jesus mentioned His pending suffering and death to the disciples, Peter pushed back, not wanting His world to crumble. Many today would have expressed the same feelings. The reason Jesus responded so dramatically was because Peter questioned the very words and will of God, just as Satan would do. After the Resurrection, Peter would understand the answer to his question. Until them, he had to trust in the One he had just confessed.

Took: What creates the gap between your confession of Christ and actual trust? What would help you trust when you want to question?

PASSAGE 121

Winning at Losing

READ: LUKE 9:23–27, SEE ALSO MATTHEW 16:24–28
AND MARK 8:34–9:1

HOOK: Why do Christians expect a better life on earth than even Jesus experienced?

BOOK: Jesus wanted to prepare His followers for the same intimidation and suffering He endured on earth. He used the wordplay of *save* and *lose* to demonstrate that nothing compares to following His example of serving others. Just as Jesus was rewarded by the Father, so will His faithful followers be.

TOOK: What have you worked to gain that God may view as loss? What should you be losing in order to win?

PASSAGE 122

A Glimpse of Glory

READ: MARK 9:2–8, SEE ALSO MATTHEW 17:1–8
AND LUKE 9:28–36

HOOK: How do you think believers or unbelievers can be flippant toward Jesus?

BOOK: Imagine the awe that gripped the disciples as they glimpsed the glory of the Eternal Lord that had been veiled by His flesh. They wanted their world to stop right there so they could enjoy the experience longer. This insightful moment would strengthen their faith as future events unfolded and would motivate them to sacrificial service. How were they able to identify Elijah and Moses, whom they had never seen? Could it be that in eternity your character and person will be self-evident? Even the Father spoke from heaven to help them understand. What a picture of eternity!

TOOK: Can you think of ways to glimpse God's glory even now? How should His glory shape your choices?

Passage 123

Shadows Before Glory

Read: Mark 9:9–13, See also Matthew 17:9–13 and Luke 9:36

Hook: Why does the fact that Jesus had to suffer confuse people?

Book: After witnessing the glory of the Transfiguration, the disciples could not comprehend Jesus' comments about *resurrection, death, and suffering*. Just like John the Baptist, who came in the spirit of Elijah, Jesus would be rejected and abused.

People fail to realize that the path to glory often goes through the shadows of pain and sacrifice. If Jesus had to endure suffering, can you expect less?

Took: How do the shadows prepare you for the glory?

Passage 124

Faith in Yourself

Read: Mark 9:14–29, See also Matthew 17:14–20
and Luke 9:37–43

Hook: When was the last time you were unable to solve a big problem? What limited you in your search for an answer?

Book: Jesus returned to the disciples to find them frustrated at their inability to cast out the evil spirit plaguing this boy. Jesus reminded them that it required belief. Evidently, they were relying on their own ability rather than faith in God to solve the problem. That is why Jesus pointed them to *prayer*. In the humble act of prayer you both acknowledge your inability and plead for God's capability. The hurdle is getting past your denial that you are trusting in God when in reality you are depending on yourself.

Took: How does trusting yourself instead of God reveal itself in your life? How could you practice more faith through prayer?

Passage 125

Paralyzing Fear

Read: Mark 9:30–32, See also Matthew 17:22–23 and Luke 9:43–45

Hook: Can you think of a time when you heard such startling or confusing news that you had difficulty absorbing it?

Book: Evidently, the disciples had such preconceived ideas on how future events would unfold that they could not process this second prediction of the Lord's death and resurrection. Their perceptions were locked on Jesus' succeeding, ruling, and inviting them to help, not on suffering.

Why do you think they were *afraid* to ask Jesus about it? Were they fearful of what might happen to them? The very fact that Jesus spoke these words should have given them confidence.

Took: How do your fears reveal selfishness? How should you react when scary news comes your way?

Passage 126

Choose Your Battles

Read: Matthew 17:24–27

✣

Hook: Can you think of time when you engaged in a conflict and later wished you had abstained?

Book: Since Jesus was God's Son, He should have been exempt from paying the temple tax, but He did so to prevent it from becoming an issue. The opposition was so desperate for a charge to pin on Jesus that they would later falsely accuse Him before Pilate of teaching against paying taxes. The Lord's compliance kept the focus on the real issue—their failure to accept the One the Father had sent. Their refusal to believe revealed itself in questions like this on taxes.

When people raise senseless concerns with you, always look for the real issue lingering in the background. Choose your battles wisely.

Took: What conflict are you struggling with today? What do you think are the real issues in the background?

Passage 127

The Race to the Bottom

Read: Mark 9:33–37, See also Matthew 18:1–5 and Luke 9:46–48

Hook: How do people play the comparison game, trying to show themselves better than others?

Book: Do you think the disciples did not grasp Jesus' predictions about His pending suffering and death because they were too busy competing for prominence? Jesus rebuked their arrogance by wrapping greatness around humble service to a child. The Lord modeled daily that humility is a race to the bottom, not the top. In God's Kingdom, the goal is to *be the very last and the servant of all*. Surprisingly, when you arrive at the bottom, you discover that you made it to the top!

Took: Why is racing to the bottom a foreign concept to most people? In which area of your life do you need to change direction?

Passage 128

A Competitive Spirit

Read: Mark 9:38–41, See also Luke 9:49–50

Hook: Which type of person do you tend to criticize that others accept?

Book: The disciples assumed this man was wrong because he was not one of them. Jesus let them know that anything done in His name is more than acceptable—it will be rewarded. Jesus is not making a point about theology or spirituality but about service. He wants you to celebrate even the most humble efforts of others done in His name.

Took: What do you think drives this competitive spirit? Can you think of someone you should criticize less and compliment more?

Passage 129

Playing Tag with Sin

Read: Matthew 18:6–14, See also Mark 9:42–50

Hook: Can you think of a person whose sinful choices affected you?

Book: Sin is contagious! When you influence others to sin, you incur the wrath of God on your life. Jesus warned His followers to take drastic steps to stop this cycle. You can influence others in two ways. Passively, your poor choices may grant them permission to do the same. Overtly, you may engage people to participate in sinful ways. To the joy of His Father, Jesus invested His life to stop this evil game.

Took: What are some ways you may push people in the wrong direction? What would you identify as a contagious sin in your life?

Passage 130

When Someone Hurts You

Read: Matthew 18:15–20

Hook: Why are people afraid to deal with those who hurt them? How do you tend to respond when someone hurts you?

Book: Holding people accountable has become a lost art. Jesus outlined a three-stage process for dealing with people who sin against an individual. First, go in private. Second, take others who have witnessed the sin. Third, take it before the larger group. Jesus knew that dealing with such problems early would lessen the impact on both those involved and the church community. He assured them of the Father's presence as they walked this path.

Took: How could accountability be like a healing salve to a soul?

Passage 131

Over-The-Top Forgiveness

Read: Matthew 18:21–35

Hook: What limits do people place on their forgiveness of others?

Book: Peter must have been the student with his hand always in the air to interact with the teacher. Jesus flipped his question about generously forgiving someone *seven times* into a dramatic teaching moment. Peter soon discovered that the astronomical number resulting from seventy sevens meant that he should not limit forgiveness with any number. In fact, as the parable indicated, he must be willing to search his heart to discover how he can forgive in the same way he wants to be forgiven.

Took: When people hurt you, how could you demonstrate that you have adopted the Lord's perspective on forgiveness? With whom do you need to start?

Passage 132

Invisible Rejection

Read: Luke 9:51–62, See also Matthew 8:19–22

Hook: Can you name a significant opportunity that you missed in life because it was overwhelmed by lesser priorities?

Book: Jesus could have expected blatant rejection by the Samaritans since they disliked all that Jerusalem meant to the Jewish people. It was the rejection of these three potential disciples which was surprising. The Lord used strong language to expose the control that hidden pressures had on their lives. Subtle things, such as physical comforts, time, and family, can divert us from following Jesus completely. These pressures probably prevented the three men from experiencing the opportunity of a lifetime, since Jesus sent out *seventy-two others* in Luke 10:1.

Took: Which priorities in your life are turning your desire to follow Jesus into subtle rejection? What needs to change to turn invisible rejection in your life into visible dedication?

PASSAGE 133

Family Pressures

READ: JOHN 7:2–9

HOOK: Which expectations from relatives do you resist the most?

BOOK: The brothers of Jesus were anxious to go to the *Feast of Tabernacles*, since it would be a popular and well-attended event where Jesus could display that He really is the Messiah. This is odd, because the brothers *did not believe in Him*. Jesus resisted, since it was not the *right time* to reveal Himself to the nation. The timing for that would wait for His prayer in the garden the night before He died. Even good people who love you can push in some wrong directions.

TOOK: What motivates friends or relatives to impose pressures like this on you? What would help you to see past the pressure to God's timing and will?

Ministry in Judea and Perea

Passages 134–192

Passage 134

Mixed Reviews

Read: John 7:11–31

⁂

Hook: Why do people respond to the same event differently?

Book: When Jesus finally arrived at the Feast of Tabernacles, He amazed even the toughest critics with His teaching. As you read the passage, look at the varying responses, and try to discover a connection between the person and their opinion. Jesus declared that an accurate understanding of Him flows from a heart that seeks to *do God's will*. Your assessment of Jesus' teaching makes a big statement to Him about your heart.

Took: What surprises you about some of the responses you have in your own heart about Jesus? What do you see in this episode that helps you understand Jesus better? What would change if you focused the review on you, not Him?

Passage 135

Power Styles

Read: John 7:32–44

❦

Hook: How do people exercise personal power in positive or negative ways?

Book: While the religious leadership was abusing its power behind the scenes to harm Jesus, He went front and center to reveal the true source of His power, the Holy Spirit. Jesus used the procession of the high priest to get water for the altar during the feast as an opportunity to introduce the future empowering of the Holy Spirit as *streams of living water*. Can you see the freshness and power in the imagery of a stream? In contrast to what the leaders were trying to do in the shadows, the power of the Spirit will bring beauty, refreshment, and momentum to all who drink.

Took: What does the Lord's example reveal about the Spirit's style? How can you keep yourself from adopting human power styles?

PASSAGE 136

Blinding Bias

READ: JOHN 7:45–52

HOOK: How does a person act when his mind is already made up about something?

BOOK: The religious leaders were infuriated at the failure of the guards to arrest Jesus. They ridiculed the soldiers who made positive comments about His teaching and even put down one of their own, Nicodemus, when he spoke up. Bias blinds people to the facts so much that they are willing to abuse both their enemies and friends. Lust for power or position makes choices take on a selfish distortion.

TOOK: What tempts you to be blind with bias at times? How is this blindness hurting a relationship in your life?

PASSAGE 137

Mean People

READ: JOHN 7:53 THROUGH 8:11

HOOK: What is the meanest thing someone has done to you?

BOOK: The way this woman was treated went beyond unfairness—it was mean. She was probably set up. The man was given a pass, and the entire matter was made public in order to trap Jesus in debate. They would abuse her to accomplish their selfish goals. The trap merely exposed their agenda, so they had to walk away. Jesus did not condone the woman's sin but considered the unfairness and responded with truth and grace. While they demanded retaliation, Jesus longed for restoration.

TOOK: How do you use subtle meanness to accomplish your desires? Have you hurt someone who needs some grace? What do you learn about grace from this episode?

PASSAGE 138

Light of the World

READ: JOHN 8:12–20

HOOK: How do you feel when a person forces you to defend yourself?

BOOK: The religious leaders repudiated the Lord's claim to be *the Light of the world* because He testified for Himself. Jesus responded that His knowledge was greater than theirs and that even the Father witnessed to His character. (Remember His baptism?) Not only had they ignored all the miracles and teaching of Jesus, they also revealed that they did *not know the Father*. Jesus must have tired of defending Himself before people who refused to see the Light sent by the Father.

TOOK: What is it about light that turns people off? What are they really saying when they make people of the Light defend themselves?

Passage 139

Life without Consequences

Read: John 8:21–30

⚜

Hook: How do people gloss over their mistakes or sins?

Book: While being rejected, Jesus raised the issue of sin. He said they would *die in their sins*. Some *put their faith in Him*, but others would not understand His true identity until He was on the Cross, where even the Father would speak and confirm their relationship. Jesus tied His identity and mission to the forgiveness of sin, but they showed little interest. They must have felt so secure in themselves that they could ignore, even kill, the Son of God. They showed no concern for the consequences coming for their sin.

Took: How has callousness to sin hardened modern culture and even the church? Which sins do you tolerate in your life?

Passage 140

Fooling Yourself

Read: John 8:31–47

❖

Hook: How do people fool themselves regarding their spiritual condition?

Book: Every religious group has people who fail to practice what they preach. These leaders claimed to be sons of Abraham, but their actions proved them wrong. They confused their family ties, religious activities, or lust for power with true spirituality. Even today people enforce their selfish demands on others. Not only do they reveal themselves as *illegitimate children*, but they ignore the truth that *will set people free*. Refuse to be bound by those who want to control you. Deception lurks in familiar places!

Took: Can you name an area in your life where you think more highly of yourself than you really should? What is the price of fooling yourself?

Passage 141

Greatness Perspective

Read: John 8:48–59

Hook: Which people in your life would you associate with greatness? Why?

Book: Jesus used their great spiritual father, Abraham, as a testimony to His own greatness. He claimed that *Abraham rejoiced at the thought of seeing His day* and that He existed before Abraham. They refused to accept the greatness of Jesus because it would diminish theirs before others. The Lord's eternal glory has ramifications. It makes human glory pale in comparison and gives Jesus the awe He deserves. Any greatness you claim must be viewed in light of His eternal person. It should motivate you to *keep His word*, which is difficult for those caught up in their own greatness.

Took: How would a focus on God's greatness instead of your own bring significance to your life?

Passage 142

Beyond the Pain

Read: John 9:1–7

❦

Hook: What unfairness in your life will not be fully understood until you get to heaven?

Book: After the disciples unfairly judged this blind man, Jesus jumped in with clarity and grace. His blindness occurred *so that the work of God might be displayed in his life*. Can you imagine enduring all that suffering so that Jesus could walk by and reveal Himself as *the Light of the world*?

When unfairness or hurts happen in your life, God is not in the dark. He knows, cares, and wants to do something beyond your imagination. He will use your pain to bring His light to you and those you love.

Took: When you suffer, what practical things could you do to help yourself and others see beyond the pain to His light?

PASSAGE 143

Neighborly Indifference

READ: JOHN 9:8–12

HOOK: Which words would best describe the relationship you have with your neighbors?

BOOK: Through the years, these neighbors became so indifferent to the blind man's plight that they did not even recognize him after the healing. How can people who are so close be so distant from each other? The Sovereign Lord places people together as neighbors to help each other. Unfortunately, people are so consumed with themselves that they miss opportunities to love and celebrate those God has placed in their path.

TOOK: How would your neighbors know that you are not indifferent but truly care?

Passage 144

Thin Loyalty

Read: John 9:13–34

⚜

Hook: When did someone throw you "under the bus" to protect himself?

Book: Even though an unmistakable miracle had occurred in his life, the healed man found little support from either his family or the religious leaders. His parents feared being *put out of the synagogue*, while the leaders struggled to protect their positions. Again, the poor blind guy was labeled as a sinner from birth (verses 2 and 34). Where is the joy or gratitude over this healing? People even called Jesus' good actions "bad" to protect themselves. What greater act must Jesus do to deserve loyalty?

Took: Why is loyalty often so thin? How would your loyalty encourage another person?

PASSAGE 145

Blind Vision

READ: JOHN 9:35–41

⁂

HOOK: Why are people often blind to the obvious truth right under their noses?

BOOK: Both the healed blind man and the critics had difficulty understanding the truth revealed to them by Jesus. Eventually, the healed man believed while the critics refused. Their jealousy prevented them from accepting Jesus as *the Son of Man*. Jesus opened this man's eyes both physically and spiritually so that he could see Jesus better than the religious experts could. The Lord takes joy in opening blind hearts. If you have doubts about Jesus, ask Him to reveal Himself to you. He has and He will!

TOOK: How does spiritual blindness affect the people you know? What would they need to see in you to see the Lord?

PASSAGE 146

The Good Shepherd

READ: JOHN 10:1–21

HOOK: When were you last taken advantage of by others? How does injustice make you feel like even God may not care?

BOOK: In His discourse on the Good Shepherd, Jesus compared Himself to religious leaders who acted like *thieves* and *hired hands*, abusing people to get their own way. Unlike Jesus, they would hurt and *destroy* others to protect their position. A good leader will *lay down his life for his sheep*. The words and actions of Jesus overflowed with love and sacrifice for people. The selfishness of others should remind you to depend on the loyal care of Jesus.

TOOK: What do you enjoy most about the Good Shepherd's care for you? How could you imitate the Good Shepherd?

Passage 147

The Few

Read: Luke 10:1–16

Hook: Why do you think most people fail to take serving God seriously?

Book: Jesus created people to do His work. Just imagine how the disciples' appointment and preparation must have thrilled them to serve. The world was their oyster, and the worst they could experience was rejection—which really was a rejection of the Father. Unfortunately, most people think they serve God more than they actually do. The fear of painful rejection or ridicule makes people smile at others instead of serving their spiritual needs. For Jesus, was rejection a sign that He was serving well?

Took: Why are these words of Jesus true in most generations: *The harvest is plentiful, but the workers are few*? What would keep you motivated to be one of the few?

PASSAGE 148

Bumping into Pride

READ: LUKE 10:17–24

HOOK: When did your exhibition of pride embarrass you in some way?

BOOK: Jesus introduced the disciples to the pitfalls of pride. In their excitement over successful ministry, they needed to be humbled by the fact that they were simply forgiven sinners themselves. Their position and power was a gift. Jesus stressed humility as the gateway to greater knowledge and service in the future. In fact, past servants of the Lord longed to see these days of Jesus to witness the fulfillment of so many promises.

You should be humbled that God would choose to use you. Taking credit only diminishes your success.

TOOK: What is the proper response when you see the Lord use you successfully? What kind of glow does humility put on your service?

Passage 149

The Good Samaritan

Read: Luke 10:25–37

Hook: Can you think of reasons why Christians find it easier to preach than to practice what they believe?

Book: Jesus had little time for people who professed knowledge of God but failed to reach out to suffering people. He flipped this test question, "*Who is my neighbor?*", to explain the real issue: *Am I a neighbor?* True knowledge will create in you a lifestyle that sacrifices to show mercy. How do you see this distinction between knowing and doing portrayed in the parable?

Took: How can knowledge become a barrier to reaching out to the needs you see daily? How could you better link the gaining of Bible knowledge with action?

Passage 150

Choosing the Best

Read: Luke 10:38–42

Hook: Looking back, what were some of the best and worst priority choices you made in life?

Book: The conflict between Mary and Martha illustrates the priorities people bring to life choices. Jesus wanted Martha to know that some things can be more critical in life at certain times. Mary could do housework anytime, but hearing Jesus was the chance of a lifetime. Daily routines can consume you at the expense of the spiritual. Even spiritual activities can become a substitute for genuine faith and life change.

Took: What does your calendar tell you about your spiritual priorities? What has been pushed aside that needs attention?

PASSAGE 151

Prayer Boldness

READ: LUKE 11:1–13

HOOK: What expectations linger in the minds of Christians when they pray?

BOOK: After teaching this prayer, Jesus encouraged His followers to pray boldly. If a father will disturb His sleeping family to lend some bread, how much more will the Heavenly Father open the door to those who knock? He commends persistence. Like a father who wants to give good gifts to his children, the Father will grant you the very best, even the Holy Spirit. So pray boldly, being assured that God will answer with something good.

TOOK: Why do you think Jesus encouraged persistence when God knows what you need before you ask? How is God's desire to give *good gifts* a nice filter for your prayers?

PASSAGE 152

Cheap Shots

READ: LUKE 11:14–28

HOOK: What is the worst untrue thing someone has said about you?

BOOK: Since all else failed, Jesus' opponents used their trump card—a personal attack. Could they have said anything worse than calling him satanic? Even the illogic of Satan casting out his own demons did not disrupt their jealousy. Jesus proved His character by this miracle, but people with an agenda still slandered Him. Their personal attacks merely revealed their evil character because true followers *hear the Word of God and obey it.* Cheap shots ricochet to say something about those who speak them.

TOOK: How could you peer through untrue accusations in order to discover truth? Why is obedience to God's Word critical to surviving cheap shots?

Passage 153

Patience in Rejection

Read: Luke 11:29–32

⚜

Hook: How are good people either ignored or rejected in today's culture?

Book: The wickedness of that generation was so great that they refused to accept Jesus as Messiah even though He proved His deity by His miracles. Their rejection was deeply entrenched. Therefore, they would receive no more signs until Jesus was raised after three days like Jonah. Even Jonah and Solomon had followers, but their superior—Jesus—was condemned by this crowd. He made it clear that eternity would expose who was really rejected by God. One day every knee will bow and every tongue confess that Jesus Christ is Lord. Patience!

Took: Why are Christians surprised by rejection when it happened even to Jesus? How could you practice God's patience when rejection comes your way?

PASSAGE 154

Eye Drops

READ: LUKE 11:33–36

⚜

HOOK: What blinds people to the truth about others?

BOOK: Jesus used the eye as an illustration for filtering truth about Him. His opponents had biased perceptions that blocked their ability to see His true identity. Their dirty eyes squinted when exposed to His light. Bias comes in many forms. For these leaders it was a matter of pride and jealousy. They saw Jesus as a threat to their powerful positions before the people. If they had used spiritual eye drops, they could have enjoyed His person and teaching, which *completely lights* the soul.

TOOK: What bias in your eye blinds you to the truth about yourself and God's designs for your life? How would cleansing your eyes from bias light up your life?

Passage 155

Too Much Religion

Read: Luke 11:37–54

❧

Hook: Which religious practices tend to confuse you? How can some traditions fool people about their true spiritual condition?

Book: Each accusation of Jesus revealed the leaders' emphasis on external rules, which disguised their lack of internal conformity. They could fool people but not Jesus, who knew their need for genuine faith. The saddest part is that they *hindered those who were entering* Christ's way.

Took: Why do people even bother with religious practices when they don't really believe? Can you identify traditions or opinions in your life that may be hindering the spiritual growth of others?

Passage 156

Justice for Critics

Read: Luke 12:1–12

Hook: When have you been criticized for your Christian stance?

Book: As Jesus' popularity with the people swelled, so did His critics. To prepare His disciples to face adversity, He assured them that the God who cares for insignificant sparrows would certainly be there for them. His followers were to remain faithful in difficult times, knowing that God would both judge the critics and provide guidance for His followers through the Holy Spirit. Even though you cannot control your critics, remember that God is in control.

Took: What are some practical ways to demonstrate your dependence on the Holy Spirit as you endure criticism? How does the coming judgment of God on your critics change your thinking?

Passage 157

The Poverty of Riches

Read: Luke 12:13–21

⁂

Hook: Can you think of a time when you felt encumbered by owning too much stuff?

Book: In response to this greedy question, Jesus revealed the emptiness of possessions. When people trust things for security instead of God, they will eventually be sadly disappointed. The Lord desires that you use your life and possessions to store up wealth in heaven, not on earth. When possessions have no eternal purpose, they lead to the worst poverty.

Took: What does being *rich toward God* imply for your life? How could you handle your finances so that it is obvious that your trust and security is in the Lord?

Passage 158

Financial Planning in Reverse

Read: Luke 12:22–34

Hook: How is today's culture obsessed with food, clothes, and possessions? How does this obsession affect your walk with God?

Book: In the days of Jesus, the common person struggled to meet daily needs like food and clothing. The typical response of worrying would not change the situation but only accentuate a lack of faith in God's ability to provide. Jesus proposed a reversal in their thinking. Instead of being consumed with material things, *seek His kingdom, and these things will be given to you as well.* When you focus on God's priorities, He grants what you need.

Took: What do you need to reverse in your financial planning and spending? How would this reversal advance your spiritual walk with God?

PASSAGE 159

Getting Motivated

READ: LUKE 12:35–48

❖

HOOK: How do Christians become apathetic in their walk with God?

BOOK: As the days approached for His death, resurrection, and ascension into heaven, Jesus prepared His followers to anticipate His return. Like this servant who had been given responsibility for the master's affairs during his absence, you should order your life as if Jesus could return any moment. When He returns, Jesus will hold you accountable for what He has given you to oversee. On that day, you will be grateful you were faithful.

TOOK: What has Jesus given you to manage in His absence? What should you be doing to get a great performance review?

PASSAGE 160

Family Divisions

READ: LUKE 12:49–53

HOOK: Can you think of a time when your loyalty to Jesus hurt a family relationship?

BOOK: The purpose of Jesus' coming was to bring peace, but it brought division because of the unbelief of some. Even families sometimes divide over faith in Jesus. This must have added stress for Christ as He anticipated His own baptism of suffering through death.

TOOK: When tensions result from your belief in Jesus, how could you lessen the strain without compromising your faith? How could you reveal love in the process?

PASSAGE 161

Missing the Obvious

READ: LUKE 12:54–59

HOOK: Can you think of a person who is successful in life but oblivious in some basic area?

BOOK: Jesus criticized the people for being able to read weather signs in the sky while refusing to see the obvious facts about Him. Everything about His life and work pointed to His true identity as God's Son. Like people who fail to take advantage of negotiating a settlement before facing a tough judge, their callousness would place them in jeopardy. Ignoring obvious truth has consequences.

TOOK: Can you think of a scriptural mandate that you skip over? Why do you ignore it?

Passage 162

Claiming Innocence

Read: Luke 13:1–9

Hook: Which failures do you tend to see in others but not in yourself?

Book: A grand display of pride is to judge others for what you are guilty of yourself. This crowd tried to read God's judgment into the tragedy suffered by others. Jesus flipped the conversation into a warning about judgment that will come to them unless they humble themselves to bear fruit by repenting and believing in Him. Instead of gloating about others, you should get serious about faith and purity in your own life.

Took: Why do people enjoy talking about the failures of others? What hypocrisy exists in your life right now that you condemn in others?

PASSAGE 163

When Rules Rule

READ: LUKE 13:10–17

HOOK: What policies that are unfriendly to people have you observed in organizations?

BOOK: The synagogue ruler rebuked Jesus for healing this woman on the wrong day. The man-made Sabbath traditions were more important to him than her health. Jesus pointed out that this ruler would change the rules for donkeys but not for a suffering woman. Often, rules and traditions reveal a person's heart and hypocrisy. Could this leader have been jealous of Jesus' ability to heal? When you hear someone celebrating a man-made rule, you should wonder why. God's rules will always help people.

TOOK: What makes you so callous that you would willingly abuse people in order to enforce a rule or tradition? What should be the purpose of healthy traditions or rules?

PASSAGE 164

Think Big

READ: LUKE 13:18–21

HOOK: Which trends in society tend to deflate a Jesus follower?

BOOK: Jesus encouraged His followers to look beyond the critics to see the unstoppable power of His Kingdom. Like a small seed that produces a large tree or a tiny amount of yeast that affects the whole loaf, His Kingdom will have an impact beyond its size and will attract many people. Never underestimate God's ability to do big things through you.

TOOK: What would help Christians think big when society makes them feel small?

PASSAGE 165

Deity Matters

READ: JOHN 10:22–39

HOOK: How do people fail to take the deity of Jesus seriously today?

BOOK: The religious line in the sand is the deity of Jesus. His claims made this crowd in the temple want to stone Him, while others believed His miracles confirmed He was God's Son. To those who believe, He promised to *give eternal life* and to protect them since *no one can snatch them out of His Father's hand.* Accepting the reality that Jesus is God grants believers security and hope in their faith.

TOOK: How could you daily remind yourself that Jesus is Lord? How could His deity shape your daily choices?

PASSAGE 166

Time Will Tell

READ: JOHN 10:40–42

HOOK: When has time proved you right about someone or something?

BOOK: When a crowd gathered around Jesus near the Jordan River where John had preached, they realized that John's testimony about Jesus had been proven true by His miracles. Their questions and misconceptions turned to faith. Following God's teaching may feel risky at times, but truth eventually prevails. Just ask John.

TOOK: Why does it often take time for someone to "get it" about Jesus? What should you be doing during the wait?

Passage 167

The Last Will Be First

Read: Luke 13:22–30

Hook: What surprises do you anticipate in heaven?

Book: A big surprise will be who actually is in heaven. Jesus' response to this question revealed the reasons why various people won't be there. Some procrastinate in believing (verse 25), others refuse to abandon their evil ways (verse 27), and many will depend on their religious heritage instead of faith (verse 28). These religious people assumed they were the *first*, guaranteed heaven, but will actually be the *last*. Those outside their circle whom they considered the *last* will be *first* because they believed. This is self-deception of the worst kind.

Took: What do you learn about eternity from this passage? Who needs your help to become one of God's first?

PASSAGE 168

A Broken Heart

READ: LUKE 13:31–35

HOOK: When did you feel rejected by someone you loved?

BOOK: Jesus *longed to gather* the children of Israel together in faith as a hen does her chicks. But they *were not willing*. One day, after the Great Tribulation, Jesus will return to earth to see some finally cry out, "Blessed is He who comes in the name of the Lord." During the Millennium, Jesus will have the enduring relationship with the chosen people of Israel that He intended. As with His nation, Jesus is patient with you. Simple obedience will keep you under His wings.

TOOK: What encouragement do you gain from the way Jesus handled rejection? What do you miss when you break His heart?

Passage 169

The Way Up is Down

Read: Luke 14:1–14

Hook: When were you given a great lesson in humility?

Book: Since Jesus put aside so much glory to come to earth, it saddened Him to see pretense and pride in others. He revealed His own spirit when He admonished the guests to take the lesser seats and the host to invite the unwanted. In God's Kingdom, the way up is down. The Lord's repayment will be worth more than any sacrifice you make. Jesus proved that *those who humble themselves will be exalted.*

Took: Why do people sacrifice the reward of heaven for acknowledgment on earth? How could you help others see that the way up is down?

PASSAGE 170

When God Gets Angry

READ: LUKE 14:15–24

HOOK: Does it surprise you that God gets angry? What would ignite His anger?

BOOK: Like this earthly host, the Heavenly Father becomes angry when people refuse to come to His banquet because they reject His Son, Jesus. The party was intended for Israel, but their failure to believe opened the door to people from around the world.

Your excuses may sound reasonable to you but reveal a disdain for your Creator and Savior. You fool yourself into thinking that earthly desires could compare to God's design for your life. No wonder God becomes angry when you choose your way over His.

TOOK: What causes you to be so arrogant that you choose your priorities over God's? How could you become angry at the same things that anger God?

Passage 171

Getting What You Pay For

Read: Luke 14:25–35

⚜

Hook: Which bumps on the Christian journey frustrate believers the most?

Book: Jesus used several metaphors to drive home the cost of following Him faithfully—family relationships, personal sacrifice, building a tower, and going to war. The result of paying the price is the opportunity to permeate society like salt for the Lord. Followers who are not scared away by the cost will discover that the fulfillment of making an impact in lives more than compensates for the sacrifice. Jesus knew that many would only want to take and not give back. If they only knew that they would get more than they pay!

Took: How does counting and paying the cost of following Jesus make life more satisfying?

Passage 172

Making God Smile

Read: Luke 15:1–32

Hook: What brings joy to the heart of God?

Book: Jesus told these three parables to deal with misconceptions about God. His detractors reasoned that Jesus could not be from God because He associated with *tax collectors and sinners.* Just the opposite is true. The Father *rejoices* when sinners come home to Him. The first two stories reveal God's passion to find the lost, while the story of the Prodigal demonstrates the vastness of His patience and grace. If that is the heart of God, it is no wonder He celebrates when you repent and help others do the same.

Took: What do the shepherd, woman, and father teach you about your Heavenly Father? What change in you would make the Father smile? How could you help others find their way home to God?

PASSAGE 173

Money Talks

READ: LUKE 16:1–15

HOOK: Why do people tend to be secretive about their financial donations?

BOOK: Jesus told this unusual parable to teach His followers to be *shrewd* in handling their finances before God. This is critical since it reveals a person's trustworthiness and real master in life. Like these religious leaders, people can *justify* themselves and forget that *God knows the heart.* Greed simply indicates that people value what is *detestable in God's sight*. This explains why so many clam up about their giving to God. They fear money talks!

TOOK: Why do you think Jesus was so forthright about financial stewardship? What would you like your money to say about you?

Passage 174

Going Casual

Read: Luke 16:16–18

Hook: Which biblical topics do believers tend to ignore the most?

Book: The root difference between Jesus and His adversaries was their attitude toward Scripture. While everything Jesus and John taught aligned with *the Law and Prophets*, these leaders had a casual and self-serving approach demonstrated by their attempts to force their way into heaven apart from faith in Jesus. Their only option was to justify themselves (verse 15). Obedience is never casual.

Took: What results come from a casual approach to God's teaching? How would you know that you are taking His truth seriously?

PASSAGE 175

Eternal Destinies

READ: LUKE 16:19–31

HOOK: Why is death such a delicate topic for some people?

BOOK: Jesus wanted all to know that earthly choices have eternal consequences. Death should only be feared by those who reject God's teaching. This parable shows that God is fair, there are no second chances, and God's Word tells what is needed to get to heaven. God never stuttered, whether He spoke through Moses, the Prophets, or the resurrection of Jesus. They all point you to faith in Him.

TOOK: Why do people ignore God's clear teaching about death and eternity? How does this parable prepare you to face death?

Passage 176

Protecting Others from Sin

Read: Luke 17:1–10

Hook: Can you think of someone who encouraged you to do something that you regret today?

Book: Since temptations constantly abound, the Jesus follower would be foolish to encourage new believers to sin in any way. Instead, you should protect others from sin by modeling great faith like a mustard seed and doing your Christian duty like this servant did. Your example can motivate others to reject sin and crave obedience, and it is the Christian's *duty*.

Took: If you considered purity and service as simply doing your duty, how would it enrich and change your life?

PASSAGE 177

Purposeful Delays

READ: JOHN 11:1–16

HOOK: When were you ever impatient or frustrated with God's timing?

BOOK: Just imagine how this family must have agonized over Jesus' delay in coming. Only Jesus knew the purpose was to cause the disciples to fully believe in Him before He entered Jerusalem the final time. The death and resurrection of Lazarus would not only bring faith to His followers but anger and jealousy to His adversaries. Even though the Lord's delays may not be always understood, they are never without a spiritual purpose.

TOOK: The next time God's schedule differs from yours, how should you respond?

PASSAGE 178

Wake Up

READ: JOHN 11:17–44

HOOK: When someone you love dies, what thoughts journey through your mind?

BOOK: Mary and Martha simply asked for a healing, but Jesus wanted to reveal Himself as *the Resurrection and the Life*. At this wake, when the guest of honor literally woke up, it empowered others to wake up spiritually. As Jesus headed to Jerusalem to die, He gave the hope of resurrection to stir His disciples' faith and calm their fears. The resurrection power Lazarus experienced at death is one you can enjoy daily for strength as you obey the Lord's words.

TOOK: If you really believed Jesus is the *Resurrection and the Life*, how would it wake you up?

Passage 179

Jealousy Corrupts

Read: John 11:45–54

⚜

Hook: How does a jealous person make life difficult for others?

Book: The response to the miraculous raising of Lazarus was split—some believed while others became more jealous. These leaders feared losing their position and power with the Roman government if Jesus' popularity spread. When jealousy trumps truth, senseless things happen. Religious leaders *plotted* to kill an innocent man. The corruption of power usually begins with jealousy.

Took: Proverbs 27:4 asks, *Who can stand before jealousy?* How can you withstand the corrupting power of jealousy when it floods your soul?

PASSAGE 180

Taken for Granted

READ: LUKE 17:11–19

HOOK: Can you think of someone's kindness that you have taken for granted? What do the simple words "thank you" say about a person?

BOOK: This group of ten lepers illustrated the different responses Jesus was getting from the people. Most were ungrateful and unbelieving, and a portion of the few who believed were outside the Jewish faith. Even though Jesus did exactly what these men wanted and needed, they callously went on their way, assuming they deserved their gracious gift. The story would have been so different if they had simply acknowledged the Gift Giver.

TOOK: Why are people so prone to be grace takers instead of grace givers? What practices could you adopt to prevent you from taking people for granted? Who comes to mind?

PASSAGE 181

Price of Procrastination

READ: LUKE 17:20–37

HOOK: When did you ever pay a price for putting off doing the right thing?

BOOK: Because the religious leaders rejected Jesus, His earthly reign was postponed. Both He and the people would suffer as a result of their failure to believe in Jesus as Messiah. The return of Jesus after the Tribulation will be similar to the days of Noah and Lot since there will be a judgment determining who may enter the Kingdom. Failing to believe God and taking matters into your own hands only brings pain for you and others. Contrary to popular thinking, instant obedience beats instant gratification.

TOOK: Where are you paying a price in your life for your failure to trust God? How does your procrastination hurt others?

Passage 182

Asking God

Read: Luke 18:1–8

Hook: When did you ever feel that your prayer request was too trivial for God?

Book: Jesus stated that the purpose of this parable is that people *should always pray and not give up*. Even though this widow had a desperate personal situation and a callous judge, she wore him down with her asking. Jesus encouraged His followers to ask. Jesus wanted to make it clear in this story that the Father welcomes your persistence. By refusing to give up, you remind yourself and the Lord that you trust Him with your situation.

Took: What affect does persistence in prayer have on you as you pray?

Passage 183

Praying with a Mirror

Read: Luke 18:9–14

Hook: When has God been silent in response to your persistent prayers?

Book: While the previous parable exhorted His followers to bring their requests to the Father, this one gave a hint why God may not respond at times. When people take the Pharisee's stance of pride instead of the tax collector's humility, they bring bad motivations, ask for the wrong things, or think that God owes them something. The principle the Lord gave was straightforward: *Those who humble themselves will be exalted.*

Look into the mirror of your prayers to see if they reflect pride or humility. When God doesn't change the situation, maybe He wants to change you.

Took: What does a proud stance in prayer say about you? Can you think of an unanswered prayer that needs some humility?

Passage 184

The Big Marriage Problem

Read: Matthew 19:1–12, See also Mark 10:1–12

Hook: What major struggles do marriages face today?

Book: Since marriage and divorce is a sensitive and divisive topic in any era, these religious leaders tried to *test* Jesus in front of the people to gain support. His response quoted the original sources in Genesis 1:27 and 2:24 before stating the real issue—*hard hearts*. Hardening your heart toward God and a spouse does many things. It willfully ignores God's clear teaching, focuses on self-satisfaction, drags others into sin, hurts innocent people, and tarnishes the witness of Christ. Like these Pharisees, you can argue, justify, or blame, but the core issue is a disobedient heart.

Took: What could you do to keep your heart soft and sensitive in your marriage or any special relationship?

Passage 185

Learning from a Child

Read: Mark 10:13–16, See also Matthew 19:13–15 and Luke 18:15–17

Hook: How do you think adults could improve their relationships with children?

Book: During this display of the disciples' harshness to the children, Jesus reacted and used the simple trust of a child to illustrate the faith response everyone must have in Him. It is easy for preconceived ideas or theological discussions to hinder people who are seeking to know the Lord. It is never complicated to enjoy and serve God.

Took: Why do you think Jesus loved the simple trust of children? How could you crawl up into His lap in pure faith to enjoy His blessing?

PASSAGE 186

Chasing Stuff

READ: MATTHEW 19:16–30, SEE ALSO MARK 10:17–31
AND LUKE 18:18–30

HOOK: How do people try to find fulfillment apart from submission to Jesus?

BOOK: Do you think this man was really able to obey this list of commandments? He chose to justify himself because he was not about to leave his wealth and follow Jesus. Enjoying his passions and possessions blinded him to true satisfaction in life. Jesus promised eternal rewards, which would overwhelm any sacrifices made to follow Him. One day people will wish they had chased the right things.

TOOK: Why does chasing stuff appeal to you more than future rewards? What do you need to rearrange in your life and how would it transform you?

PASSAGE 187

Payday Jealousy

READ: MATTHEW 20:1–16

HOOK: Why are salaries such a sensitive topic among coworkers?

BOOK: Jesus gave this parable in the context of Peter's previous question: *What then will there be for us?* (Matthew 19:27). The Lord wanted them to know that faith goes beyond service, to trusting God to be fair with His rewards. The all-knowing and just God will be generous. Only the mind and heart of God could nuance all the factors in computing eternal rewards. This parable reveals the jealous and competitive spirit that disqualifies a person to judge others. Your role is to be faithful and trust God to do what is right.

TOOK: Why does jealousy make people doubt the fairness of God? How should God's generosity toward others change your attitude?

Passage 188

Reading Is Believing

Read: Luke 18:31–34, See also Matthew 20:17–19 and Mark 10:32–34

Hook: When did you last get frustrated repeating yourself to someone before the person finally understood?

Book: In this third prediction of His death and resurrection, Jesus made it clear that all the prophecies in the Old Testament about Him would come true. Even though the disciples still did not understand, it would be clear to them soon. The same guarantee applies to the unfulfilled prophecies concerning future events and the Lord's return—they will come to pass as written. Unfortunately, too many people fail to believe what they read in the Bible.

Took: Why do many followers of Jesus basically ignore Bible prophecies? What was God's purpose in being so emphatic about the future?

Passage 189

Path to Glory

Read: Mark 10:35–45, See also Matthew 20:20–28

Hook: Can you think of ways you seek prominence at the expense of other people?

Book: James and John had no idea of the suffering involved in their request. The other ten disciples had the right to be *indignant*. But none of them really understood that the path to glory comes by serving others, as Jesus would demonstrate on the Cross. There is no other path to greatness since *even the Son of Man did not come to be served, but to serve*. Jesus wants His followers to ignore the tendency of human rulers and follow His humble path to greatness. This path may make little sense to you now, but is the only one that brings you to glory.

Took: Why do you think Jesus chose to demonstrate His glory with sacrificial service?

PASSAGE 190

Simple Faith

READ: MARK 10:46–52, SEE ALSO MATTHEW 20:29–34 AND LUKE 18:35–43

HOOK: How do people make faith in Jesus complicated?

BOOK: The irony in this event is that a blind man taught people with sight how to see Jesus. On His way to Jerusalem to be rejected and crucified, Jesus was refreshed by the genuine faith of blind Bartimaeus. What does simple faith look like? Bartimaeus acknowledged the true identity of Jesus as the Messiah, *Son of David*; demonstrated *faith* by His request; and then began the journey to *follow Jesus*. The simplicity of faith is blinding to some people.

TOOK: How have you complicated your walk with God? What changes would return you to simplicity?

Passage 191

Faith Changes

Read: Luke 19:1–10

Hook: What lifestyle changes would you expect when someone becomes a follower of Jesus?

Book: Even though the Jewish people despised Zacchaeus as a tax collector for the Romans, he taught them how to be a true *son of Abraham*. He went out on a limb to seek Jesus and then demonstrated His faith with genuine life changes. Can you really be a Jesus follower if your repentance has no fruit? When God changes your heart through faith, it should trickle down into all areas of life. Thankfully, real faith is catalytic.

Took: After believing, Zacchaeus knew he needed to make some financial restitutions. Which areas of your life need to change to better reveal your faith in Jesus and restitution to others?

Passage 192

The Waiting Game

Read: Luke 19:11–27

❖

Hook: Can you think of a time when you failed to take advantage of a great opportunity?

Book: Jesus gave this parable to teach His followers how to maximize their service while His Kingdom was delayed. Since a mina was worth about one-fourth of a year's salary, each person was given significant responsibility until the newly appointed king returned. Like these people, Jesus' followers have been given responsibilities for which He expects accountability. You have resources, abilities, and spheres of influence where He anticipates faithfulness until He returns. The waiting game provides you the opportunity of a lifetime.

Took: What has Jesus placed in your hands to use for Him until He returns? What are you waiting for?

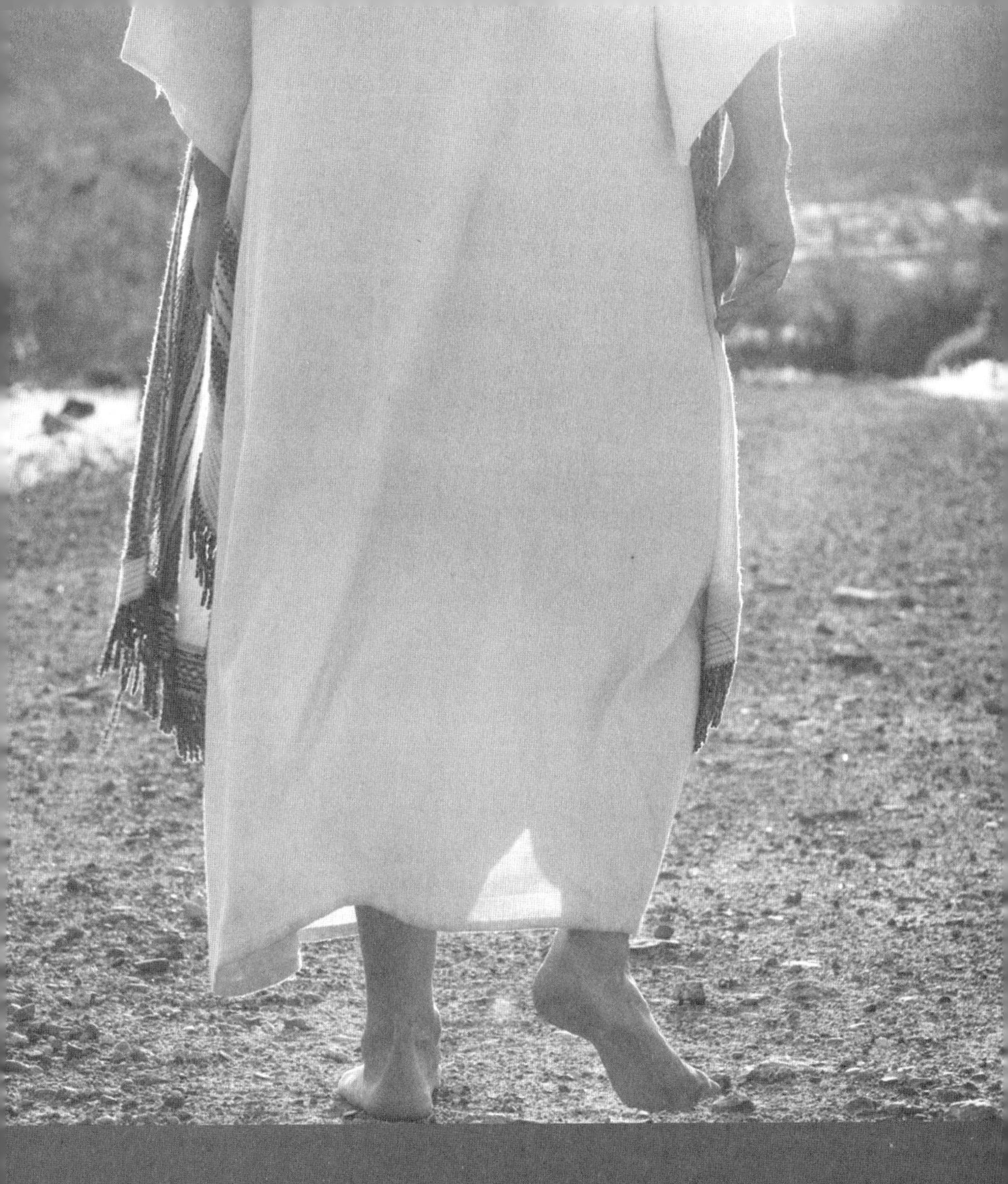

Final Days in Jerusalem

Passages 193–239

Passage 193

People with an Agenda

Read: John 11:55–57

⚜

Hook: When were you ever disappointed by a religious leader?

Book: The excitement of the people for Jesus was overshadowed by the jealousy of these religious leaders. Instead of dealing with His message of righteousness and love for others, they plotted to eliminate Him. They lost their spiritual mission and became obsessed with keeping their positions. Since Jesus was too much competition, He had to go.

When you lose sight of God's agenda, you quickly become absorbed with your own. Personal agendas tend to be self-serving and petty.

Took: What would indicate that a leader may have a personal agenda? How could you test your agenda to ensure that it comes from God?

Passage 194

Facing Rejection

Read: Luke 19:28–44, See also Matthew 21:1–17, Mark 11:1–11 and John 12:12–19

Hook: When have people turned on you after you helped them?

Book: During the triumphal entry into Jerusalem, Jesus offered Himself as the *Lord* and *Messiah*, knowing He would be rejected. In a few days, these same crowds would cry out for His crucifixion. The nation would not only pay a horrible price when the Romans destroyed Jerusalem in A.D. 70, but will suffer until Christ returns one day. Even after Jesus gave the people healing, food, and wonderful teaching, they still followed angry people and their own self-interests. If people treat the perfect Son of God like that, can you expect less?

Took: Why do you tend to be surprised by rejection? What does rejection reveal in you and others?

PASSAGE 195

Fake Fruit

READ: MARK 11:12–14, SEE ALSO MATTHEW 21:18–19

HOOK: When were you tricked into thinking something fake was genuine?

BOOK: This fig tree was a symbol of the nation of Israel, which enjoyed the appearance of religion but lacked the evidence of genuine spiritual fruit. By rejecting Jesus, they would be rejected themselves and judged by God. A fraudulent heart can easily hide behind pious words or religious activity. Real spirituality comes by believing Jesus and obeying His words. Who is real or fake is obvious to the One who counts.

TOOK: What do you think are indicators of false or true godliness today? How would you like to demonstrate the genuineness of your faith?

Passage 196

Quick Changes

Read: Mark 11:15–18, See also Matthew 21:12–13 and Luke 19:45–48

Hook: What bothers you about church life or organized religion?

Book: Jesus cleansed the temple at the beginning of His ministry and now again at the end. The leaders had too much invested in selling sacrificial animals to pay attention to God's purpose of *prayer* and teaching. This *den of robbers* was even willing to *kill* Jesus to sustain their operation. Do you think Jesus could have used any other strategy? Evidently, some things are so outrageous to God that instant change needs to happen.

Took: What change in your church, small group, or family would renew spiritual passion the most? Act quickly!

Passage 197

Light at the End of the Tunnel

Read: John 12:20–36

Hook: When did you need hope in a season of trouble?

Book: As the antagonism mounted in Jerusalem, Jesus again predicted His death while both giving and receiving hope. His message of hope to the people was to trust in the Light while they had the chance. The Father then gave hope to Jesus, who was feeling the pressure of the Cross, by endorsing Him from heaven. No matter how desperate life appears, God always provides light at the end of your tunnel. That light is usually found in His Word and His priorities.

Took: Why is it so easy to overlook the light of Jesus so that *darkness overtakes you*? When darkness comes, what should you do?

PASSAGE 198

Seeing the Father

READ: JOHN 12:36B–50

⚜

HOOK: What do you think causes the mixed responses to Jesus today?

✓

BOOK: The responses to Jesus in this passage are typical. Many *would not believe* in Him, while some of those who did *would not openly acknowledge their faith for fear* of the Pharisees. Why do people respond so differently to Jesus? He made it clear that those who believe see *the One who sent Me*. Believers see the Father in Jesus and hear the ring of heaven in His words. Jesus pointed people to the Heavenly Father with His words and His works. For those who saw, the result was faith and eternal life.

TOOK: What are some specific ways people could see the Heavenly Father through you?

Passage 199

God Is Able

Read: Mark 11:19–25, See also Matthew 21:19b–22 and Luke 21:37–38

Hook: When did you last doubt God's ability by taking matters into your own hands?

Book: Jesus used Peter's astonishment at the curse on the fig tree to teach him a lesson about prayer. If Jesus has such miraculous ability, He has the power to answer prayer. The two demands He makes are to have *faith in God* and *forgive* others. The dramatic language Jesus used in the passage illustrates well His ability to act on your behalf.

Took: Why do you think Jesus linked faith and forgiveness as requirements in prayer? How would these elements strengthen your trust in God's ability?

Passage 200

Refusing to Get It

Read: Matthew 21:23–27, See also Mark 11:27–33
and Luke 20:1–8

Hook: What drives a person to ignore the facts and stubbornly refuse to believe in Jesus?

Book: Sometimes the question is also the answer! *The things* that Jesus did demonstrated His authority and could only come from one source, God. The religious leaders' question confirmed the facts of Jesus' identity, and their refusal to answer His question revealed their stubborn hearts. Believing that Jesus came from heaven would demand that they submit to His authority and relinquish their own. No way! Stubborn refusal always has a motive.

Took: How does your stubbornness bump into Jesus' authority? What drives your refusal to "get it" at times?

Passage 201

Fooling Yourself

Read: Matthew 21:28–32

Hook: Can you think of ways practicing religion can fool you about your actual spiritual stance?

Book: Like the second son in the parable, Israel had the appearance of saying "yes" to God but failed to come through with the obedience that demonstrates true faith. Even the faith of the people they despised, *tax collectors and prostitutes*, did not stir jealousy to motivate them to *repent and believe*. Failure revealed their self-deception.

Took: Why is obedience an indicator of true faith in Jesus? Can you think of ways you are fooling yourself?

Passage 202

Running Out of Patience

Read: Matthew 21:33–46, See also Mark 12:1–12 and Luke 20:9–12

Hook: Why do you run out of patience with others?

Book: This parable revealed the limits of God's patience with the nation's historical refusal to receive His message through the prophets. They would even do the worst—kill His Son. Since the Father's patience has run out, *the kingdom of God will be taken away from them and given to a people who will produce its fruit*. Jesus will build His new church from all nations of the world. For a time, the church will enjoy the affection of the Father and do His work. The Father is more gracious than you can dream, but His patience has limits. Jesus is still waiting for the day when Israel will acknowledge Him.

Took: How are you testing the patience of God?

PASSAGE 203

Banquet Blues

READ: MATTHEW 22:1–14

HOOK: What do you think would *enrage* the Heavenly Father the most?

BOOK: This third consecutive parable revealing the nation's rejection of Jesus portrayed the Father's anger and His turning to focus on the Gentiles, whom Israel despised. The church would begin on the Day of Pentecost and do Christ's work until He returns. After all the eternal preparations for this banquet, it is no wonder the Father gets upset at the excuses people make not to attend. Seating is limited to people who show themselves worthy by faith in Jesus.

TOOK: What excuses do people make today for refusing to celebrate God's Son? What do these excuses say to the Father?

Passage 204

Traps Backfire

Read: Matthew 22:15–22, See also Mark 12:13–17
and Luke 20:20–26

Hook: When did someone try to trap or embarrass you for his or her own gain?

Book: Since the Pharisees wanted to eliminate Jesus, they had to fabricate a charge. Since the *Herodians* sided with the Romans in collecting taxes, they were taken as witnesses to hear Jesus' answer to their question. They assumed His yes or no would incite someone, either the people or the Romans. Jesus could see through these *hypocrites*, and He surprised them with His answer. Whenever others try to trap or manipulate you, they reveal their character.

Took: What tactics do you see in the Pharisees that indicate manipulation? What do you learn from Jesus about responding to people who try to trap you?

Passage 205

Dealing with Ridicule

Read: Matthew 22:23–33, See also Mark 12:18–27 and Luke 20:27–40

Hook: How can theological or religious conversations degenerate into ridicule?

Book: In an effort to prove their belief that there was no resurrection, the Sadducees asked Jesus a question dripping with mocking ridicule. Jesus responded with Scripture, indicating that the eternal promises to Israel demanded the patriarchs be alive in the future. Then Jesus pointed out the real issue: *You are in error because you do not know the Scriptures or the power of God.* He responded to their ridicule with the clear teaching of Scripture, revealing their ignorance of God and His Word. Who *astonished* whom?

Took: Why are the facts the best weapon against ridicule? Can you think of ways you engage in ridiculing other followers of Jesus?

PASSAGE 206

The Bottom Line

READ: MATTHEW 22:34–40, SEE ALSO MARK 12:28–34

⚜

HOOK: How do people add to God's expectations of them?

BOOK: The competitive spirit of the Pharisees drove them to ask another question to trap Jesus and to exonerate them. Unfortunately, the answer revealed that their treatment of Jesus and others broke both of these *commandments*. Following Jesus is not complicated. Everything you read in the Bible boils down to two basic commands: *loving God* with all your heart and *loving your neighbor as yourself*. Since God's bottom line is no secret, you know exactly what to do.

TOOK: Why does God's bottom line, these two commands, make so much sense? Why is it so difficult?

Passage 207

Jesus Is Lord

Read: Matthew 22:41–46, See also Mark 12:35–37
and Luke 20:41–44

Hook: How do people, knowingly or not, treat Jesus as less than Lord?

Book: Jesus turned the tables on the leaders and asked a question to reveal that He is more than the Son of David; He is the Son of God. Even King David referred to the coming Messiah as *Lord*. Since the discussion of lordship would vindicate Jesus and expose the unbelief of the leaders, they went silent. Trusting the lordship of Jesus changes everything.

Took: How do you gloss over the lordship of Jesus in your life? How would trust in Jesus as Lord change your style?

Passage 208

Best Leadership Practices

Read: Matthew 23:1–12, See also Mark 12:38–40 and Luke 20:45–47

Hook: Which traits in leaders tend to disappoint you?

Book: After exposing the spiritual bankruptcy of the religious leaders, Jesus turned to warn the people. He exposed their desire for prominence and their failure to *practice what they preached.* Like Jesus, they should have been serving the people with humility.

The lust for power, control, and prominence tends to haunt leaders. Jesus could have had all that and more but chose to *humble Himself* as a *servant*. Why not learn the best from the Best?

Took: Who needs spiritual leadership from you? Which best practices of Jesus do they need to see in you?

Passage 209

Slamming Heaven's Door Shut

Read: Matthew 23:13–39

Hook: How do religious people sometimes discourage others from following Jesus?

Book: The hypocrisy of the religious leaders was so uncaring that it even *shut others out of the kingdom of heaven*. Jesus pronounced seven woes on them, predicting their future judgment. Their kind will not respond to God's grace until the second coming of Christ, when their distress is so great that they call out, *"Blessed is He who comes in the name of the Lord."* The saddest part is that their unbelief and anger took others with them.

Took: What does the Lord's strong language indicate about such leaders? What do you see in your life that may harm the spiritual life of others?

Passage 210

Putting Others to Shame

Read: Mark 12:41–44, See also Luke 21:1–4

❖

Hook: Whose spiritual walk has made you rethink your own?

Book: The devotion of this widow stood in stark contrast to the hypocrisy of the religious leaders and other worshipers. Her sacrificial gift demonstrated true faith since it represented *all she had to live on*. Evidently, position or wealth is not necessary to impress the Lord. Her act of dependence must have encouraged Jesus as He faced rejection from others.

Took: What did her gift say about this widow? How could your dependence on the Lord stand out to others?

Passage 211

Bringing on Suffering

Read: Matthew 24:1–14, See also Mark 13:1–13 and Luke 21:5–19

Hook: What kinds of choices tend to bring suffering into your life?

Book: This passage begins the Olivet Discourse, which answered the question: *What will be the sign of your coming and of the end of the age?* Jesus' answer revealed the terrible events and suffering that will accompany the first half (verses 4–8) and the second half (verses 9–14) of the Tribulation period. If the nation had accepted Jesus as their Messiah, they would have saved themselves and future generations much pain. Choices have consequences.

Took: How are you or those you love suffering because of poor choices? How can you learn from consequences to help you make better and godly choices?

Passage 212

The Worst Is Yet to Come

Read: Matthew 24:15–25, See also Mark 13:14–23 and Luke 21:20–24

Hook: Why does suffering grab your attention and cause you to seek God?

Book: By referencing Daniel 9:27 Jesus placed these events in the middle of the Tribulation period, when the Antichrist breaks his peace treaty with Israel and unleashes the worst events the world will ever see. Even then, God will step in to soften the blow for believers living at that time. The good news is that this season of worldwide horror softens the heart of Israel to welcome Jesus as their Messiah.

Took: Why do people often choose to learn the hard way? How has your stubbornness or failure to trust God caused you pain?

Passage 213

The Second Coming of Jesus

Read: Matthew 24:26–31, See also Mark 13:24–27 and Luke 21:25–27

Hook: Can you think of an event in your life that made you happy while it made others sad?

Book: When the Lord *will gather His elect* from one end of the heavens to the other, *all the peoples of the earth will mourn* at Jesus' return. One person's joy is another's judgment. The cosmic displays will make His coming unmistakable. The redemption and promises that Jesus offered at His first coming will be completed at His second. He will make good on all His promises, to the dismay of unbelievers.

Took: What do you think will dazzle people the most when Christ returns? How does this blessed hope strengthen you to face the pressures from an unbelieving world?

Passage 214

Be Alert

Read: Matthew 24:32–41, See also Mark 13:28–32 and Luke 21:28–33

Hook: Can you remember a time when you were surprised by an event because you were not alert? Why did you miss it?

Book: Anticipating that people will become overwhelmed by the terrifying events of the Tribulation period, Jesus used the metaphor of the *fig tree* to warn people to look for the signs of His Second Coming. Like the people in *Noah's* era, it is easy to become so consumed with life that you ignore coming judgment. Unlike the Rapture, at this Second Coming unbelievers are the ones taken away, but to judgment. If you fully comprehended the future and the holy demands of God, you would definitely be alert to make different choices.

Took: What would spiritual alertness look like in a believer?

Passage 215

Expectations

Read: Matthew 24:42–51, See also Mark 13:33–37 and Luke 21:34–36

Hook: How have you been affected by others' neglect in their work or life?

Book: Even though God's calendar for future events is unknown to you, there is something you can know for certain. God wants you to serve Him faithfully until Jesus returns. When the Lord returns, His expectations are very clear. Since believers are stewards of His work on earth while He is away, He anticipates seeing them busy and faithful. Even though personal abilities and spheres of influence may differ, God's expectations are the same for everyone.

Took: What is your responsibility from the Lord until He returns? Who would be affected by your faithfulness?

Passage 216

Self-Deception

Read: Matthew 25:1–13

Hook: How do people fool themselves into thinking they are more mature spiritually than they really are?

Book: The failure of the five virgins to be prepared in this parable illustrates a lack of genuine faith in Jesus. They possessed the religious forms (*lamps*) but not the necessary faith. (*Oil* is often a metaphor for the Holy Spirit.) The other five virgins were prepared for the bridegroom's return because they took him at his word and responded with faithfulness and obedience, as believers should to Jesus. Self-deception only feels good until reality hits.

Took: How does self-deception creep into your life? How can you maintain a realistic view of your walk with God?

Passage 217

Faithfulness Rewarded

Read: Matthew 25:14–30

Hook: How well did you do with the largest responsibility ever given to you?

Book: Anticipating His death, Jesus informed His followers that Kingdom responsibilities would be left in their hands until He returned. This parable stressed that responsibilities are distributed to *each according to his ability* and that faithfulness is expected. Could the master's response be a picture of heaven? Commendation: *Well done.* Eternal responsibilities: *I will put you in charge of many things.* Joy: *Share your master's happiness!* The Lord will reward the return you provide on His investment in you.

Took: What *well done* commendation would you like to receive from the Lord when you see Him?

Passage 218

Look Over Their Shoulders

Read: Matthew 25:31–46

Hook: Can you think of a time when the efforts you intended to help someone spilled over and touched others as well?

Book: Jesus ended this discourse on end times with concrete ways to demonstrate faithfulness while He is away. Even a cup of water given in His name will be rewarded. Why? Because *"Whatever you did for one of the least of these brothers and sisters of Mine, you did for Me."* If you look over the shoulder of everyone you serve, you will see Jesus, because every sacrifice you make for someone is really an act of love and worship to Him. People are not a problem but a pathway to the heart of God.

Took: How could you sharpen your vision to see Jesus standing behind hurting people?

PASSAGE 219

Jesus Knows

READ: MATTHEW 26:1–5, SEE ALSO MARK 14:1–2 AND LUKE 22:1–2

HOOK: When did you last sense from someone's attitude that things were not right between the two of you? What tipped you off?

BOOK: While Jesus was finishing His Olivet Discourse predicting His pending death, the religious leaders were plotting His demise in another part of town. They were trying to be sly, but He knew exactly what they were doing. Being God, Jesus knows everything pertaining to His life and yours. But knowing didn't make Him run or scheme in return. Thankfully, He also knew the great results the pain would bring. When you feel hurt or alone, remember that Jesus knows.

TOOK: Since Jesus knows, how should you respond when people plot against you?

PASSAGE 220

The Fragrance of a Life

READ: JOHN 12:1–8, SEE ALSO MATTHEW 26:6–13 AND MARK 14:3–9

HOOK: How has the sacrifice of another person captured your imagination?

BOOK: Mary was so overwhelmed after Jesus raised her brother, Lazarus, she had to express her thankful heart with this sacrificial gift and act. Her passion did not go unnoticed because *the house was filled with the fragrance of the perfume*. The good, bad, and ugly in this story were all exposed to her devotion. The fragrance of her sacrifice touched everyone from Jesus to Judas. Never underestimate whom the Lord might reach through the fragrance of your loving sacrifices.

TOOK: Why do you think the Lord stated in Matthew 26:13 that *wherever this gospel is preached throughout the world, what she has done will also be told in memory of her?*

Passage 221

When the Target Is You

Read: Luke 22:1–6, See also Matthew 26:14–16 and Mark 14:10-11

Hook: When have people plotted to do evil toward you? What was their goal and strategy?

Book: When *Satan entered Judas* to betray Jesus, he gave away some of his strategies. Here, he used jealous leaders, secrecy, financial gain, manipulation, friendship, and treachery. The list should not be surprising because Satan's style hasn't changed since the Garden of Eden. Satan's goal is to control and gain power or adulation. When you see someone abusing a righteous and innocent person, recognize the abuser's desperate agenda to gain something. Of course, it all backfired at the Cross!

Took: How does your desire to control prompt you to do unfair things to people in your life?

Passage 222

Funeral Arrangements

Read: Luke 22:7–13, See also Matthew 26:17–19 and Mark 14:12–16

Hook: What kinds of emotions did you sense when making funeral arrangements for a loved one?

Book: Since Jesus would soon die as the final Passover Lamb for the sin of the world, the symbolism of this Passover must have stirred His emotions. His impending death would satisfy the righteous requirements of the Holy God once and for all. Instead of making a yearly Passover sacrifice, people could now trust Christ for forgiveness of sin. It is no wonder that Jesus had to guide these Passover preparations since forgiveness is the work of God. He prepared for His own death so that you might believe and live.

Took: Since service and sacrifice take planning, what arrangements do you need to make in your life?

PASSAGE 223

Bragging Rights

READ: LUKE 22:14–16, 24–30

HOOK: Why is boasting both so popular and senseless?

BOOK: Jesus wanted His disciples to know that their bragging rights were not valid. On the eve of His death, their arrogance contradicted what He was doing. For Jesus it was all about serving others, not Himself. That is why He came as a Servant, not a *King*. Since the *Kingdom* would be in their hands after His soon departure, He wanted them to understand that spiritual *greatness* comes to the *one who serves*. Understanding how the Kingdom works was essential to service.

TOOK: Why does being a servant instead of a king make sense in God's Kingdom? How do servants brag?

Passage 224

Washing Feet

Read: John 13:1–20

Hook: What specific act of humility has someone done for you?

Book: Knowing that His time on earth was coming to an end, Jesus wanted to show His followers the *full extent of His love* by washing their feet and going to the Cross. His humble act revealed a path to dealing with sin. First, everyone must have a spiritual bath by faith (verses 8–11). Second, you should deal with your daily sin through confession (verse 10), and then help others with their sin as well (verses 12–17). Each of these practices demands a bold step of humility.

Took: Why is humility necessary when dealing with personal sin? What are the differences between celebrating but not following the humility of Jesus?

Passage 225

The Judas Friendship

Read: John 13:21–30, See also Matthew 26:20–25,
Mark 14:17–21 and Luke 22:21–23

Hook: Why does betrayal in a friendship surprise us? How does it hurt?

Book: *Jesus was troubled in spirit* because He knew that one of His friends was on the verge of betraying His love and friendship. When He offered the piece of bread to Judas, it was a token of intimate friendship, His invitation to remain loyal. When Jesus admonished him to *do quickly* his evil deed, He revealed His personal commitment to the Father's purposes, even in this treachery. It is amazing how the Lord used Judas' betrayal to make many future loyal friends with Jesus.

Took: When the betrayal of a friend hurts you deeply, how would Jesus long for you to respond?

Passage 226

A New Commandment

Read: John 13:31–38, See also Matthew 26:31–35, Mark 14:27–31 and Luke 22:31–38

Hook: What words would people outside the church use to describe those on the inside?

Book: Jesus gave this new commandment of love, which was really a forgotten one buried under the pile of traditions. Just before His arrest, He wanted His followers to know that love must govern all they say and do. Love distinguished Jesus in His ministry and the way He treated both Judas and Peter in this episode. But His greatest love was accepting the pain to *glorify the Father* and bring forgiveness to the world. Your mandate is to love others *as He has loved you*.

Took: What does love bump into when it tries to control your choices? How would love change your relationships?

PASSAGE 227

Grace Dementia

READ: MATTHEW 26:26–29, SEE ALSO MARK 14:22–25 AND LUKE 22:17–20

HOOK: Which memento do you treasure to remind you of a special person in your life? What memory does it rekindle?

BOOK: By instituting the Lord's Supper, Jesus provided a tangible way to remember the significance of His death. He used two common elements at the table: *bread* to symbolize His body and the *cup* for His shed blood, which provides forgiveness from sin. From Jeremiah 31:31–34 you know that the fulfillment of this new covenant will be completely realized with Israel after the Second Coming. Until then, you can participate by enjoying forgiveness through faith in Him. Jesus wants you to remember!

TOOK: Why can people go long periods of time forgetting Christ's sacrifice for mankind? In addition to the Lord's Table, what could jog your memory to cure grace dementia?

PASSAGE 228

A Portrait of Heaven

READ: JOHN 14:1–4

❧

HOOK: What are some common misconceptions about heaven?

BOOK: To soften the blow of His impending death, Jesus provided a glimpse of heaven to quiet their *troubled hearts*. As in an ancient wedding, Jesus was going to His *Father's house* to *prepare rooms* for those who trust Him, His bride; and then He will *come back* to take them to the eternal home. He wants His followers to be where He is. One day, at your death or at His return, Jesus will take you to be with Him (see 1 Thessalonians 4:13–18). For Jesus, death was the path home to be with the Father. He said heaven is for those who *trust in God and trust also in Him*.

TOOK: What do you discover about heaven from this passage? Why does the hope of heaven bring peace to troubled hearts?

PASSAGE 229

Going Home

READ: JOHN 14:5–14

HOOK: Why do thoughts of "going home" to your roots capture your imagination?

BOOK: Where was Jesus going? His answer provided ultimate truth for mankind. He came from the Father, revealed the Father, spoke the words of the Father, enjoyed oneness with the Father, glorified the Father, returned to the Father, and is the *way* to the Father. Going home to the Father who loves Him provided the hope Jesus needed to face the Cross. Since you were created to enjoy the Father and Jesus provided the path back home, real meaning in life is discovered by trusting and shaping your life around that joy.

TOOK: When did you trust in Jesus as *the way and the truth and the life*—your path home? Why does this hope outlast everything else?

PASSAGE 230

Passing the Test

READ: JOHN 14:15–31

⚜

HOOK: What do you think would help Christians feel confident in their walk with God?

BOOK: Just before He went out the door to begin the journey to the Cross, Jesus gave the disciples this admonition: *If you love me, you will obey what I command.* He promised that the Holy Spirit would come to help them understand His words and that He would one day return from heaven to reward their obedience. The search for a secret to the Christian life ends in obedience. It reveals your *love* and brings the *peace* you covet. The Lord's submission to His Father strengthened Him to say, *Come now; let us leave.* He obediently stepped out the door to face death on the Cross to glorify His Father.

TOOK: Why do you think the Bible is the best-selling book of all time and yet one of the least read? Why did Jesus make obedience the test of love for Him?

PASSAGE 231

Closeness to God

READ: JOHN 15:1–17

HOOK: Why do people think a walk with God is difficult?

BOOK: On the path from the Upper Room to the Garden of Gethsemane, Jesus passed a vineyard and used the analogy to teach His disciples how to stay connected with Him after His death. The flow of their obedience to His words would strengthen the bond between the Vine and His branches. To Jesus it was simple: *"If you keep my commands, you will remain in my love, just as I have kept my Father's commands and remain in His love."* Closeness with God is merely a step of obedience away.

TOOK: Which things in your life look disobedient to God? Why does obedience make you feel closer to the Father?

PASSAGE 232

Behind Hate

READ: JOHN 15:18 THROUGH 16:4

HOOK: When has your faith in Jesus brought conflict or hate in someone else?

BOOK: Jesus knew that His followers would become the targets of hate-filled people. He warned: "*They will treat you this way because of My name, for they do not know the One who sent Me.*" When personal attacks don't make sense, look behind the words. Unfairness simply reveals the heart. Whether it is the crucifixion of Jesus or the attacks on the faithful, hate exposes a lack of love and obedience to the Father. When it comes your way, it verifies you know the Father and seek to serve him (2 Timothy 3:12).

TOOK: What can you learn from the Lord's response to hate-filled people?

Passage 233

Meet Your Counselor

Read: John 16:5–15

Hook: Can you remember a time when God placed someone in your life to provide wise counsel you desperately needed?

Book: On the eve of His death, Jesus reminded His disciples that they would not be left alone. The Father would send the Holy Spirit to counsel, convict, and make God's truth known to them. The same Spirit that descended on Jesus at His baptism is the Holy Spirit who would later come at Pentecost to empower believers. Every time you open God's Word, the Spirit teaches, convicts, and counsels you with truth and righteousness. You are never alone.

Took: As you read God's Word and live your life, how could you be more sensitive to the counsel of the Holy Spirit?

PASSAGE 234

Joy Robbers

READ: JOHN 16:16–22

HOOK: How did a person or situation rob you of your joy recently?

BOOK: When Jesus saw the disciples' uneasiness with His predictions about future events, He used the example of the pain and joy of childbirth to bring them comfort. Soon their pain at the Cross would be replaced with the joy of the Resurrection. Jesus knew that when they saw Him again their questions would be answered and emotions restored. Your hope of seeing Jesus one day can shape your perspective on the ups and downs in life. No question will remain unanswered then.

TOOK: If your questions will be answered and your pains forgotten when you see Jesus, how should you treat them until then?

PASSAGE 235

Asking the Father

READ: JOHN 16:23–33

HOOK: Why do Christians fail to pray as often as they should?

BOOK: Not only would the coming Holy Spirit counsel the disciples, they would enjoy direct access to the Heavenly Father when they prayed in Jesus' name. Their sorrow at the Cross would be replaced with the strength of the Spirit that would help them better sense their closeness with the Father. After the Resurrection, the disciples would be able to *take heart* because they would fully know that He had *overcome the world*.

TOOK: What are the benefits of praying in Jesus' name? How does prayer enable you to enjoy the Father's love that much more?

PASSAGE 236

Glory That Lasts

READ: JOHN 17:1–5

HOOK: Why does the applause you get from people often appear shallow?

BOOK: The famous High Priestly prayer of Jesus granted a window on glory that lasts forever. He knew that the momentary flickers of men's applause would soon be overshadowed by rejection. He longed for the glory that comes from God. Jesus deserved the Father's glory because He completed *the work* God *gave Him to do*. The anticipation of that glory motivated Him to sacrifice His life. Just think how different life could be if you filtered everything through the lens of eternal glory.

TOOK: How does the applause of people hinder seeking the applause of heaven? How could you motivate yourself to choose eternal glory?

PASSAGE 237

Prayer for Protection

READ: JOHN 17:6–19

HOOK: If you were facing death, what would you pray for those you leave behind?

BOOK: Anticipating His execution, Jesus prayed that the Father would *protect* His disciples as they now faced the *evil one*. Since their relationship began by *accepting* His words, Jesus prayed that the Father would continue to *sanctify them by the truth*. The believer's source of strength against evil is accepting and practicing God's Word. Jesus knew that only two things on earth are eternal: people and His words. He was *sent* and sends you to bring the two together. No wonder that was His passion and prayer for His followers.

TOOK: Why is the Word of God so critical to your participation in the work of Jesus? How should this prayer encourage you to pray for those you love?

Passage 238

The Attraction of Unity

Read: John 17:20–26

Hook: Why is unity such a delicate commodity in families and churches?

Book: In this section of His prayer, Jesus looked to the future and prayed *also for those who will believe*. That includes you! He prayed that future believers would so imitate the unity of the Godhead *that the world may believe*. Jesus must have felt that Christian oneness and unity would be the most powerful witness to unbelievers of His mission and the Father's glory. As you lay aside petty or selfish desires, it makes the Father *known*. Nothing attracts like unity.

Took: How could you practice unity with other believers so that it provides a clear testimony to the world?

Passage 239

Strength in a Crisis

Read: Luke 22:39–46, See also Matthew 26:36–46, Mark 14:32–42 and John 18:1

Hook: When did you last beg God for strength to endure a difficult situation?

Book: In His *anguish*, Jesus did the most sensible thing, He prayed. The Father immediately responded by sending an angel to *strengthen* Him. Twice Jesus warned His disciples to pray as well so *that they would not fall into temptation*. Instead of praying, the disciples slept, missing out on the strength the Father could have given them so that they would not have fled when the arrest occurred. Prayer is more about strengthening your dependency on God than informing Him of your needs.

Took: Why is prayer so essential to spiritual strength? How could your prayer life become more about dependence on the Father than a mere list of requests?

Betrayal, Crucifixion and Burial

Passages 240–256

Passage 240

Who Is in Control?

Read: Matthew 26:46–56, See also Mark 14:43–52, Luke 22:47–53 and John 18:2–11

❧

Hook: When did you ever feel that circumstances in your life were out of control?

Book: The large mob brought swords and clubs to control the arrest but soon discovered that they were not in charge. Even Peter tried to intervene with a sword. Jesus surprised everyone, revealing that His Father and the Scriptures would dictate events. In the midst of hatred from His enemies and betrayal and desertion from His friends, Jesus confidently trusted in God's Word, which predicted these events. Trusting the Scriptures allowed Him to place control where it belonged. The Father will never disappoint you.

Took: How would you know in a situation that you have given control to God?

Passage 241

The Style of Untruth

READ: JOHN 18:12–14, 19–23

HOOK: Why do people sometimes play dumb when they really know the facts?

BOOK: These leaders arrested Jesus because they didn't like the things He taught, and then they acted ignorant of His teaching. Their questions were merely a trap. They slapped His face because He refused to play their evil game. When people reject the truth, their style gives them away. Here they used mob rule, secrecy, entrapping questions, false witnesses, and abusive behavior. When people act unfairly, truth is not their goal. The style of untruth always reveals an agenda.

TOOK: How did Jesus model truth when confronted with untruth? How can you avoid the style of untruth?

Passage 242

Jealousy's Chaos

Read: Matthew 26:57, 59–68, See also Mark 14:53, 55–65, Luke 22:54, 63–65 and John 18:24

Hook: What motivates people to spread false rumors about others?

Book: During one night, Jesus endured six mock trials before religious or civil authorities. Unfairly, they arrested Him first and sought concrete evidence later. Their zeal to recruit false accusers only revealed their contempt and jealousy. Since they desperately wanted to put Jesus to death, they pounced on His claim to be the Son of God. Of course, this demanded that they ignore all His miracles and their own evil deeds. When things don't make sense, jealousy is usually crouching at the door.

Took: Proverbs 27:4 asks, "*Who can stand before jealousy?*" How does the chaos of jealousy manifest itself in your world? What do you learn from Jesus' response to jealous people?

Passage 243

Loyalty Choices

Read: Matthew 26:58, 69–75, See also Mark 14:54, 66–72, Luke 22:54–62, and John 18:15–18, 25–27

Hook: When is it difficult to be loyal to Jesus in the public square?

Book: Peter had boasted in the Upper Room that not even death would hinder His loyalty to Jesus. Yet before the night was over he *disowned Him three times*. Do you think Peter feared the anger and abuse being hurled at the Lord? After he witnessed the Resurrection, Peter's fear of others was replaced with allegiance to Jesus as he became a spokesman for the apostles. He quickly discovered that everything paled in comparison to the love of Christ. After all, hadn't the Lord been the most loyal to him?

Took: Why is loyalty to Jesus a pressure in your life? How would people know that you are loyal?

PASSAGE 244

Refusing Truth

READ: LUKE 22:66–71, SEE ALSO MATTHEW 27:1 AND MARK 15:1

HOOK: When have you seen someone stubbornly refuse to accept the plain facts in a situation?

BOOK: Under the cloak of darkness, this is the third trial that night of Jesus before the religious leaders. They refused to accept His teaching and miracles, which proclaimed and vindicated His true identity as the Son of God. Obviously, the facts only got in the way of their desire to eliminate Him. In their lust for status and control of the people, He was too much competition. Their refusal of the truth hurt Jesus but also revealed their motives. Callousness often provides a window on the heart.

TOOK: Why is arguing with hard-hearted people so frustrating? What does their stubbornness say about their motives?

Passage 245

Even Blood Money Talks

Read: Matthew 27:1–10

Hook: If money could talk, what would it say about the holder?

Book: When Judas *was seized with remorse* for *betraying innocent blood*, he *threw the money into the temple*, then *went away and hanged himself*. The money shouted to him about his treachery and Jesus' purity. The intensity of the money's message is seen in his suicide. The money also made a statement when the leaders purchased the *Field of Blood*, fulfilling the ancient prophecies of Jeremiah 19. Money always talks about human passion or God's faithfulness.

Took: Why does money reflect the heart so well? What do you learn about your motivations by analyzing your finances?

PASSAGE 246

On the Side of Truth

READ: JOHN 18:28–38, SEE ALSO MATTHEW 27:2, 11–14, MARK 15:1–5 AND LUKE 23:1–5

HOOK: Why is truth so crucial to healthy interactions?

BOOK: At six in the morning, the religious leaders took Jesus to the politicians for execution. His conversation with Pilate centered on *truth*, which only vindicated Him. These facts were obvious to Pilate, *"I find no basis for a charge against Him."* Truth is a divider of people. The religious leaders were more concerned about ceremonial cleanliness than telling the truth, while the "defiled" politician, Pilate, sought the facts. No wonder Jesus stated that *everyone on the side of truth listens to Him*.

TOOK: What is required of someone who wants to be on the side of truth? How does truth cleanse relationships?

PASSAGE 247

Strange Bedfellows

READ: LUKE 23:6–12

HOOK: How do people compromise themselves to gain a friendship?

BOOK: To shift responsibility for the death of Jesus, Pilate sent Him to Herod, a competing authority. The silence of Jesus so enraged Herod that He *ridiculed and mocked Him*. This unfair process toward Jesus created a friendship between the two rulers, who *before this had been enemies*. The desire for acceptance and friendship can often outweigh truth and loyalty. Both the religious and political leaders demonstrated that people may bless themselves at others' expense. Beware when strange bedfellows come together.

TOOK: Why does participation in bad behavior create a bond between people? What can believers do to protect themselves from relationships that team up to hurt others?

PASSAGE 248

The Wrath of Jealousy

READ: MATTHEW 27:15–26, SEE ALSO MARK 15:6–15,
LUKE 23:13–25 AND JOHN 18:39–19:16

HOOK: How does jealousy reveal itself in inappropriate behavior?

BOOK: Pilate wanted to release Jesus but could not stand up to the *envy* of the religious leaders. Jealousy draws out the worst in people. Here, they sided with a notorious prisoner over Jesus, ignored God's prompting to Pilate's wife, stirred up the mob to *shout all the louder*, ignored the Lord's innocence, and even let their future *children* take the punishment for their actions. Jealousy hurts, and it never makes sense.

TOOK: What do you think drives a jealous person? What impresses you about the way Jesus handled the wrath of jealous people?

Passage 249

Intentional Hurts

Read: Mark 15:16–19, See also Matthew 27:27–30

Hook: What drives people to go out of their way to hurt or insult another person?

Book: This treatment of Jesus was meant to go beyond abuse to *mock* Him and His claim to be the *King of the Jews. Again and again* they hit and insulted Him. Sometimes a mob stirs people to do things they may not do on their own. Righteousness makes a good target. People like to justify themselves by pounding good people down to make themselves feel superior. Ironically, their insults testified to the Lord's greatness and their low character. When insulted, look beyond the hurts to see the motives.

Took: What do you learn about human nature from the insults given Jesus? How can you prepare yourself for insults that may come to you?

Passage 250

The Ripples of Rejection

Read: Luke 23:26, See also Matthew 27:31–34, Mark 15:20–23 and John 19:16–17

Hook: When did rejection experienced by someone close to you spill over and touch your life?

Book: On the way to the Cross, Jesus warned the women weeping for Him that His rejection would have consequences for them and future generations. His followers in every age would face similar opposition and ridicule. The worst will come during the Tribulation (Revelation 6:15–17), when people will wish for death rather than face the judgments on earth. The ripples of rejection and judgment will continue and intensify until Jesus returns.

Took: How does the rejection of Jesus have ripples that impact your daily life? How could you thrive even in a climate of rejection?

PASSAGE 251

Ultimate Forgiveness

READ: LUKE 23:33–43, SEE ALSO MATTHEW 27:35–44, MARK 15:24–32 AND JOHN 19:18–27

HOOK: What has been the most difficult thing for you to forgive?

BOOK: As Jesus looked down from the Cross, His heart melted with compassion for those doing the unimaginable. He prayed, *"Father, forgive them."* He offered forgiveness even as they acted out their sin against Him. No one is beyond His grace. While His ultimate sacrifice was being provided for the world, His grace was received by an individual. The repentant thief demonstrated how to believe by simply trusting in who Jesus is and what He did on the Cross. Jesus invites even the worst to enjoy forgiveness.

TOOK: What do you learn about forgiveness in this passage? Write out your prayer of faith and acceptance of the Lord's forgiveness.

PASSAGE 252

Feeling Alone

READ: MARK 15:33–37, SEE ALSO MATTHEW 27:45–50, LUKE 23:44–46 AND JOHN 19:28–30

HOOK: Which circumstances in life tend to make people feel alone?

BOOK: Jesus felt *forsaken* on the Cross as He took the burden of the world's sin on His body. The pain of becoming sin for humanity (2 Corinthians 5:21) and taking the punishment that sinners deserve must have been so great that it made Him feel separated from the Father. As the only Lamb of God, He had to walk this path alone to satisfy righteousness. Yet He was strengthened to endure the Cross and would eventually sit at the right hand of the Father. When you feel alone, remember that you are not!

TOOK: What makes you feel distant from God at times? What could you do to strengthen the bond between you and the Father?

PASSAGE 253

Truth Is Obvious

READ: MARK 15:38–42, SEE ALSO MATTHEW 27:51–56
AND LUKE 23:45–49

HOOK: Why does truth rise like cream to the top?

BOOK: At the moment of His death, Jesus was vindicated by both God and man. The torn *curtain* in *the temple* demonstrated that the Father accepted His sacrifice, providing access to Him for all who believe. Then, the immediate response of the *centurion* said it all. Throughout His life, Jesus claimed to be the *Son of God* and the Mediator with the Father. These claims led to His death, but His death verified His claims. History and life would be so different if people only believed the obvious truth.

TOOK: Why is God's truth so difficult for people to accept? How should belief in God's truth embolden you?

Passage 254

Method in the Madness

Read: John 19:31–42

Hook: Can you remember a time when you perceived that God had arranged events in your life?

Book: The rush of the religious leaders to get the body of Jesus off the cross before the beginning of Sabbath helped confirm two prophecies. Like the annual Passover lamb, no *bones* were ever broken (Numbers 9:12; Psalm 34:20), and they looked *on the one they have pierced* (Zechariah 12:10). Centuries before, God spoke in detail about events on the Cross.

When you feel like madness consumes your life, remember that God already knows and is at work.

Took: What do these two prophecies tell you about the integrity of Scripture? How could you prepare yourself to better perceive God's purposes in the madness of life?

Passage 255

The Loyal Few

Read: Mark 15:42–47, See also Matthew 27:57–61 and Luke 23:50–56

Hook: Can you think of a person who stuck with you through thick and thin?

Book: Even though Joseph was a member of the religious council that persecuted Jesus, he *boldly* put his reputation in jeopardy by requesting the Lord's body. While others fled, Joseph and Nicodemus pushed fear aside in their passion *for the Kingdom of God*. Can you imagine how the Father must have felt seeing their devotion acted out toward His crucified Son?

Casual faith is just that and fails to ring the bells of heaven like these men did. Never let the fear of people rob you of honoring the Lord.

Took: Why is loyalty to Jesus something you fear at times? What kind of statement would your loyalty make to the Lord and others?

PASSAGE 256

Stopping the Inevitable

READ: MATTHEW 27:62–66

HOOK: What are some ways people try to thwart the work of God on earth?

BOOK: In spite of the ignorance they faked during the trials, the religious leaders knew quite well the teaching of Jesus, especially about resurrection. Their accusation of *deception* is really a testimony to their own style. This effort to team up with the Romans to prevent the Resurrection was futile since the purposes of God always prevail. Their failure is a reminder to always trust what God says in His Word because it always comes true.

TOOK: In which areas in your life do you try to stonewall the inevitable power of God?

Resurrection and Ascension

Passages 257–267

PASSAGE 257

Slow Learners

READ: LUKE 24:1–12, SEE ALSO MATTHEW 28:1–8,
MARK 16:1–8 AND JOHN 20:1–9

HOOK: How do you feel when people don't pay attention to your instructions?

BOOK: The angels reminded the women that Jesus repeatedly predicted His suffering, death, and resurrection. By not listening well, the Lord's followers missed the significance of the events they witnessed and the opportunity to help Jesus through it all. When God speaks, it is for your benefit, not His. The disciples would have had such a different experience if they had listened. Their failure brought heartache and confusion, but, thankfully, God repeats Himself.

TOOK: What causes spiritual dullness when hearing God's Word? How could you sharpen your listening skills?

PASSAGE 258

Blinding Emotions

READ: JOHN 20:10–18

HOOK: How can emotions make you irrational in a crisis?

BOOK: Mary Magdalene was so overcome with grief that she not only failed to grasp the significance of the Resurrection, she didn't even recognize her risen Lord. Her *crying* turned to joy when she finally recognized Him. No longer did her feelings overwhelm the facts. When feelings flow from the facts, you gain deeper understanding and fulfillment. It releases enjoyment in the ultimate relationship.

TOOK: How do the emotions that flow from knowing God's truth differ from other feelings? How do biblical emotions bring satisfaction?

PASSAGE 259

Cheating Backfires

READ: MATTHEW 28:9–15

HOOK: When were you ever caught in your own lie?

BOOK: While the Resurrection brought joy to the women, it ignited the competitive juices of the religious leaders. Since the facts surrounding the Resurrection were so obvious, their only recourse was to lie and cheat. They were no strangers to these methods. This time their deceit backfired. It merely reinforced the reality of the Resurrection and revealed their jealous motives. Their cheating has become a lasting testimony to the truth of the risen Jesus.

TOOK: Why does cheating backfire? How would people know that you are not a cheater?

Passage 260

Seeing Is Not Essential to Believing

Read: Luke 24:13–35

Hook: When did you ever doubt something until you saw it with your own eyes?

Book: These two followers were so blinded by their disappointment that they failed to recognize the risen Jesus. If they had studied the Scriptures or listened to Jesus, they would have understood. Seeing was not necessary to believe. The challenges in life may get you down because you do not know or accept the truth in God's Word. Like these two, people fail to trust God until they see confirmation after events unfold. Life would be enriched if you put believing before seeing.

Took: Why is a regular Bible-reading habit essential to trusting God? How would trusting God in advance alter your approach to life?

Passage 261

The Resurrected Body

Read: Luke 24:26–43, See also John 20:19–23

Hook: How do you think current fascination with the supernatural affects the way people view the resurrection of Jesus?

Book: This passage provides vivid details about the resurrected body of the Lord. He was recognizable, could appear suddenly, had flesh and bones, and could speak and eat. But best of all, His message was *"Peace be with you."* What the disciples thought was a scary situation actually was about peace. Jesus' resurrection was real and brought comfort because He was real—the very Son of God. Any supernatural event claiming to be from God must provide the same.

Took: How does the Resurrection shape your thinking about the supernatural? Why do you think Jesus was so anxious to reveal Himself to the disciples?

PASSAGE 262

Jesus Saw You Coming

READ: JOHN 20:24–31

⚜

HOOK: How would you like to be recognized or honored by God?

BOOK: In Thomas' struggle, you catch a glimpse of the Lord's heart: *Blessed are those who have not seen and yet have believed*. Jesus knew that people in every age who never saw His risen body would *stop doubting*, *believe*, and cry out, "*My Lord and my God*." The purpose of John's Gospel is *that you may believe that Jesus is the Messiah, the Son of God, and that by believing you may have life in His name*. Faith in Him is the only response that will grant you eternal life and more than you ever dreamed.

TOOK: How do you feel knowing that Jesus anticipated your faith? Why does faith honor the Lord? Have you placed your faith in Jesus as Savior and Lord? He saw you coming!

Passage 263

Instant Perspective

Read: John 21:1–14

⚜

Hook: Which event in your life affected your future the most?

Book: This third appearance of the risen Jesus to the disciples captured their imaginations immediately. When John saw the Savior, he cried out, *"It is the Lord!"* This prompted Peter to immediately jump into the water to rush to shore. Seeing Jesus gave them an instant perspective on life, which would change them forever. Catching 153 large fish reminded the disciples that the Lord could do great things through them if they simply obeyed and served Him. Finally, they would catch the vision of being fishers of men.

Took: How does this passage sharpen your perspective on serving Christ?

Passage 264

Second Chances

Read: John 21:15–17

❦

Hook: Which issues cause people to think that they cannot be used of God?

Book: It may not be a coincidence that Jesus gave Peter three opportunities to reaffirm His commitment since he had previously denied the Lord three times. The Lord reinstated him publicly so that others could not hold his failure against him. The grace of God overflows to anyone craving a second chance. No matter who you are or what you have done, the path home is always the same: loving the Lord and serving His people. Watch God use your second chance to grant one to others.

Took: Why is *feeding His sheep* a good test of love and loyalty to Jesus? How could you maximize your second chance?

Passage 265

Enjoying Contentment

Read: John 21:18–25

Hook: What drives people to be jealous of opportunities that come to others?

Book: After Jesus foretold the ministry and death that Peter would encounter, Peter responded by questioning the future of John. Jesus challenged him to stay focused on his own calling and to *follow Him*. Your competitive spirit can make you question the fairness of life or compare yourself to others, which only diverts you from following Christ. While His followers' common calling is helping His sheep, true satisfaction comes by accepting and fulfilling the unique role God has given each one.

Took: Why does knowing and fulfilling your role in God's Kingdom bring contentment to your soul? How does it affect your relationships?

Passage 266

Struggles with Authority

Read: Matthew 28:16–20

Hook: Why do people struggle to accept the authority of Jesus Christ?

Book: Even after His resurrection, Jesus still had doubters mixed in with His worshipers. True followers would make His last command their first concern. Participating in this Great Commission testifies that *all authority in heaven and earth* belongs to Him and that we can depend on His strength *to the very end of the age*. How can you fear or fail with all that?

Took: How could you release the authority of Jesus in your life? Why is participation in the Lord's command a good indication of your heart?

PASSAGE 267

Coming Back

READ: ACTS 1:1–11, SEE ALSO LUKE 24:44–53

❖

HOOK: How do people feel when someone mentions the return of Christ?

BOOK: Jesus responded to their questions about the future with an urgent focus on the present. He promised them the coming power of the Holy Spirit and commissioned them to take the good news to the world. The angels made it very clear that Jesus *will come back in the same way they have seen Him go into heaven*, so they needed to get to work. These Jesus Passages began with the promise of the Lord's first coming and end with the anticipation of His coming again. Since the First Advent came to pass as predicted, you should trust and prepare for the second. The best part is that He is coming back for you!

TOOK: What would you want Jesus to discover about you when He returns?

Walking Like Jesus

Whoever claims to live in him must live as Jesus did.

1 John 2:6

Congratulations! You have successfully traveled through every passage in the life of Jesus. The dream is that this journey has taken you beyond knowledge to a passion to imitate Him in every area of your life. Even small life transformations will startle others as you live as Jesus did.

Such a journey is not easy. The pressures of culture and friends may make you feel like you are turning around a barge on the raging Mississippi River. You feel restricted on both sides, and the current is flowing against you. Various thoughts go through your head.

The voices of pride pull you back into old and familiar ways. After all, you are a nice person and your opinions matter. Then, you look around and see that very few people take the words of Jesus seriously in their lives. Is it really worth the effort and sacrifice?

You are not alone. Even Jesus encountered with many pressures and rejection from those who should have understood and loved Him. His commitment to walk God's way cost Him dearly, but He never gave up. Of all people, He had the right to walk away from it all.

Deep in your heart, you know that the Jesus Passages unfold a lifestyle of fulfillment and joy like none other. The four Gospel writers were so convinced you needed to hear the words of Jesus and see His example that they made the effort to write it down. Others through the centuries have preserved His words, often at great sacrifice. There is an audience in heaven who has experienced the reality of it all and is cheering you on to read and obey.

You may be asking yourself if walking as Jesus did is even possible. After all, He was the Son of God and you are merely human, with all the accompanying frailties. Evidently, He thinks you can be successful or He would not have called you to this level of obedience or provided the necessary resources. The purpose of His teaching and life was to empower you to love God as you were created to.

When you start to live as if He is Lord, everything changes. You recognize that making it about you and your ways has taken you in many wrong directions. Instead, by doing exactly what He says and following His footsteps, you discover that you can love God and others as He did. Following Him as Lord provides a compass to guide you through the toughest challenges in life.

If this is the quality of life you covet, here is an acrostic that will equip you to walk daily as the Lord did. By memorizing and practicing this every day, you will unleash the power of God in your life so that you make a difference in the lives of others. Here is a simple and constant reminder how He can be LORD!

Love God
Obey His Words
Radiate His Grace
Depend on His Spirit

LOVE GOD

Love motivated everything Jesus did. He revealed the depth of His love for the Father when He stood to leave the Upper Room for the Garden of Gethsemane and said, "But the world must learn that I love the Father and that I do exactly what my Father has commanded me. Come now; let us leave" (John 14:31). His radical focus on going to the cross went beyond the salvation of souls to an announcement to the world of the depth of His love for the Father.

This love compelled Jesus to get up early in the mornings to spend time with His Father in prayer. Before He met the challenges of the day, He had to talk to His Father. Just imagine the conversation. It was more than mere communication; it overflowed with adoration and dependence. In the depths of His being, He longed for the relationship they once had in heaven.

Having experienced both heaven and earth, Jesus knew the love that really counted. He craved both enjoying and returning the Father's love. That is why He faced the cross so boldly. By fulfilling His mission to save people from their sins, He shouted love for His Father.

Jesus summed it up well in Matthew 22 when He was asked to name the greatest commandment. He answered with two. The first is to love God with all you are. This demands you recognize that you were created by Him for His purposes, admit that you rebelled and sinned against His holy nature, and that you believe in Jesus who died to forgive you. Just as Jesus displayed His love for God by going to the cross, you reveal your love for God by accepting through faith what Jesus did on the cross to reconcile you to the Father. Any other response is unloving toward God.

The *Jesus Passages* Journal was prepared to guide people to faith in Jesus Christ as Savior. If you are not sure that you have ever responded to the love of God by believing in Him, take the time right now to whisper a simple prayer for salvation: *Lord Jesus, I confess that I am a sinner. I trust You to save me from my sin and make me Your child. Help me to love You every day as I seek to walk as You walked.* This act of faith is God's way for you to begin to love Him His way.

The second commandment Jesus gave was to love others as you love yourself. Since God is in heaven and invisible to you, could it be that a primary way to reveal your love for Him is to love people? In fact, He said that the Law and the Prophets can be summarized by these two commandments. It appears to be almost impossible to have one love without the other.

This truth is best described in the most familiar verse in the Bible, John 3:16. "For God so loved the world that he gave his one and only Son, that whoever believes in him shall not perish but have eternal life." If God reveals His love by sacrificing for people, you imitate Him well when you do the same.

The love that Jesus and the Father shared empowered Jesus to not only tolerate the worst but to fulfill the best. He basked in the Father's endorsement, "This is my Son, whom I love" (Matthew 4:17). He knew that the opinion of the Heavenly Father was the only one that really mattered.

Jesus' love for God touched everything He did, and it will make you successful in your spiritual pilgrimage. Your challenge every day is twofold. First, you must shape your thoughts, words, and actions so that they shout love to God. Yes, it will make you feel like you are walking upstream in today's culture, but think of the statement it makes to the Father. Second, show the people in your world a fresh path as you reflect God's love to them. Walking like Jesus demands nothing less.

Does this kind of love sound impossible? Are you wondering how to stretch yourself to love this way? Just proceed to the next letter in the acrostic—

Obey His Words

Love is often perceived as an abstract concept with little teeth. Not to Jesus. He blended love and obedience into a synergy of goal and method, a harmony of dream and stance. Jesus knew that only His obedience to the Father would generate love. That explains His overwhelming passion to submit so exactly to the Father, which would display His love for all to enjoy.

Abiding in the ultimate Father and Son relationship, Jesus knew that God's words were given for His best and intended to be obeyed. Even more, in the Sermon on the Mount, He made it clear that God's words will outlast everything, even heaven and earth. Since two things on earth are eternal, God's Word and people, His obedience to one cultivated a love for the other that would last throughout eternity.

Have you ever wished that God would tap you on the shoulder to tell you what you need to know or do in order to show love? Thankfully, He does. The apostle Paul reminded young Timothy that "all scripture is God-breathed and is useful" (2 Timothy 3:16). Since the Bible provides real truth from the Ultimate Author, it seems like every time you read it the very breath of God lifts from a page to whisper His ways into your life.

The more you read the Bible, the more you realize it shares either implicit truth or guiding principles essential to traversing life's passage in this world. As you learn to walk as Jesus did, people will see changes in your style that spill over in love. When God's ways begin to saturate your soul, you will be convinced that "obey" is actually spelled "love."

The problem is that obedience comes with a price. It requires time with God in His Word. Jesus lived as if He could not begin the day until He had spent moments learning from His Father. Are you willing to create a set time in your schedule to absorb God's truth so your obedience can blossom into love? Investing in such a schedule will become the catalytic decision to release the answers, freedom, and joy you crave.

This commitment can be compared to the discovery of the "Jesus Boat" in 1986. During a drought on the shores of the Sea of Galilee, this first-century boat was exposed embedded in the mud. Raising the ancient craft was deemed near impossible since it had the consistency of wet cardboard. Carefully, scientists were able to remove the boat and place it in a chemical bath, which over time replaced the weak material of the boat with a stronger substance so that it could be displayed for all to see. Yearly, thousands of visitors are able to marvel at the display of a boat like the ones Jesus used because of this gradual and amazing transformation.

Just imagine what a biblical makeover could look like in your life. As you replace old habits with God's ways, your inner peace swells as you realize that you are pleasing and loving the One who really counts. Then, you notice that family and friends look at you differently, appreciating you more as they witness the concern and love coming their way. When your obedience starts to change everything, you will wonder why you waited so long. All you need to do is set that schedule and keep learning His Word.

Obedience will slowly but surely shape you into a person who truly makes a difference. What will this transformation look like? What kind of person will you become? Read on because the third letter in this acrostic provides a snapshot of the impact you can enjoy—

RADIATE HIS GRACE

What did the masses see in Jesus that drew them like a magnet? He had something so refreshing it compelled the people to chase Him to get even more. His style created such a rush that He often had to slip away for moments of solitude to reenergize Himself away from the masses and even His disciples. He exuded exactly what people wanted.

In that religious milieu of burdensome teachings and rules, Jesus offered freedom. The religious establishment had limited God's role to that of judge, while Jesus reopened the window on His character of love that offered grace. The people craved hearing about the true nature of their Heavenly Father, which had been distorted for too long.

They could witness the difference in all Jesus did. He offered Himself as the Bread of Life that would bring satisfaction to their souls. He invited the thirsty to drink of His streams of Living Water to enjoy the refreshment of the Holy Spirit. He lived and presented Himself as the Light of the world that would light up their lives. His style must have captured the loyalty of the woman caught in adultery when He said, "Then neither do I condemn you. Go now and leave your life of sin" (John 8:11). People could see a new day and take heart because He had overcome the world.

With the wind of the Father and the Holy Spirit at His back, He was able to set his face like a flint toward His mission, as prophesied by Isaiah. The mission outlined to Joseph before Jesus' birth was very clear: "He will save his people from their sins" (Matthew 1:21). It drove Jesus to take on flesh, become a servant, and humble Himself to the barbaric death of the cross. In life and death, He radiated with His words and His life the Father's love and grace for all to see. The brilliance did not go unnoticed.

Jesus realized that even though people could not see the Father, they could catch a glimpse by watching Him. That explains the call to His followers to be the salt of the earth and the light of the world. Just as salt preserves and light reveals, you can radiate God's righteousness as you obey Jesus' words and imitate His life. As God's Word changes your priorities, you will echo the genius of Jesus' words, "Let your light shine before others, that they may see your good deeds and praise your Father in heaven" (Matthew 5:16). Salvation for people is only granted by the Lord, but He wants to use you. If you show up living God's way, He will create the sparkle for others to see.

Before ascending back to heaven, Jesus called you to His mission with these direct words, "All authority in heaven and on earth has been given to me. Therefore, go and make disciples" (Matthew 27:18–19). Just as He invested His life in sharing God's grace, He invites you to discover that same fulfillment in pointing people to the Father. Your life is full of family, familiar people you bump into regularly, or those with special needs whom you would like to help. How will they know Christ and His wonderful grace unless you show them the way? What would it take for them to see the brilliance of His love in you?

You may wonder if the changes and sacrifices, or even criticisms, in life are worth it. The answer will be obvious on that day when you finally see the Risen Christ in all His eternal glory. Having used your opportunities to share that glory with others will be rewarded by God with radiance in you that will last forever. Deep in their hearts, people know there is something more to life but they don't know what it is. As you shine and share, God will show them the path.

Obviously, lighting up your world with God's grace takes a unique energy source beyond yourself. Read on to discover what you may have forgotten.

DEPEND ON HIS SPIRIT

Radiating God's grace with your friends or family may feel impossible in your situation, but don't worry. While in the Upper Room with the disciples on His final night, Jesus sensed their troubled hearts and confusion. He knew that they would desperately miss His leadership and strength. During the next twenty-four hours they would feel abandoned and alone, but they were not.

That night, He broke the news of the coming Holy Spirit whom the Father would send to strengthen them to continue the mission and teach them even more truth. Though they would not be able to see the Spirit, they would sense His presence and no longer feel like orphans.

The Holy Spirit would make their ministry easier by going ahead of them to convict people of sin, righteousness, and judgment. He would embolden them by unfolding future events so that they would know the end from the beginning. His constant strength and guidance would enable this small band of followers to do what they could not on their own—dramatically change the world. They would discover that the radiance flows *from* the Spirit—but *through* them.

These early followers were literally transformed by the power of the Spirit. Their fear grew into boldness that eventually faced down the opposition and spread the grace of God throughout their world. Later, in their writings, they told exactly what the Holy Spirit did to release His power in them.

Here is a list of ways the Spirit was active in the early Church and still is today:

- He indwells you when you trust Christ as Savior. He is always with you no matter what you do or where you go (1 Corinthians 6:19).
- He seals your salvation and relationship with Him forever. He will always claim ownership of you (Ephesians 4:30).
- He gifts you with spiritual abilities for ministry and empowers you as you serve others (1 Corinthians 12).
- He prays with you and blends your needs with the perfect will of God (Romans 8:26–27).
- He enables you to resist the desires of the sinful nature. His teaching motivates you to make the right choices (Galatians 5:16).
- He guides your life. He teaches you and helps you follow God's Word (Romans 8:14).

When you read the Bible and implement what it says, you release all the power of God's Holy Spirit. The transformation in your life will bring the satisfaction for which you have longed, and your radiance will capture the imagination of those you know. But, most of all, it will make the bells of heaven ring for joy.

It is no surprise that even God's own Son at His baptism welcomed the Holy Spirit to strengthen and enable Him. He knew that this power was essential for Him to complete His mission in that hostile environment. What kind of statement does that make about your need for the Spirit?

Like Jesus, darts or arrows will come your way, but He modeled that you must not face them alone. With the help of the Spirit, He was empowered to love hurtful people and make the tough sacrifices necessary for their good. From His days in heaven, He knew that in the Father's design life is always better together.

People are watching you to see if Jesus really works. Ask God to transform their curiosity into faith in Him as Lord as they see you Love, Obey, Radiate, and Depend on Him. This strategy worked for Jesus, and it will for you.

Never forget that the Lord is in the Jesus Passages waiting for you. Like the little children of old, He wants to place you in His lap, put His arms around you, and bless you. As you sit and listen to His words, watch them trickle into your life and fill you with His love. His lap is a comfortable place and you won't want to leave, but when you do, jump down and invite the people in your path to hear His wonderful words of grace. After all, the dream of the Jesus Passages is to discover how to walk like Jesus.

Challenge!

Walk through the Jesus Passages again and compare your responses from the second time with the first to see how you have matured in walking like Jesus. Thankfully, this journey never ends.

ACKNOWLEDGMENTS

As I walked this journey through the Jesus Passages, it was obvious that I was not alone. God had positioned others at pivotal junctures to help me learn what was necessary to create this journal. Since this book reflects their influence on my life, I would like for you to meet these special people I love.

Many of the insights you will read were forged in pulpits and classrooms of congregations I have served. These dear people not only listened patiently but interacted with questions and observations to enlarge my horizons. I would like to thank Electra Community Church (Texas), Shades Mountain Bible Church (Alabama), Park Bible Church (Ontario), and the Community Church at Saddle-Brooke (Arizona), for loving our family and allowing me the freedom to stretch my wings. I am indebted to two gifted administrative assistants, Cathy Fraser and Amy Malcom, who did so much of the work only to give away the credit.

It has been an honor to work with Gannett Ministries, founded by my father, and the Gannett Leadership Center in Canada. These two organizations serve together from different countries to empower leaders and individuals in their work for the Lord. Their boards, volunteers, and loyal supporters have enriched me with the prayer, finances, and encouragement necessary to create this tool for you. My prayer is that their investments will grow into a harvest of righteousness, to God's glory.

As a new author, I was delighted to discover the experienced staff at Deep River Books. The enthusiasm and gracious welcome of Bill Carmichael helped me see the potential and motivated me to press on. Kit Tosello patiently walked me through this new adventure with her insight and loving spirit, while Mary Hake faithfully used her editor's pen to make the passages more helpful for you. Their passion to build God's kingdom is infectious.

My wife and I were both privileged to be raised by loving and God-honoring parents: Alden and Georgetta Gannett, and Vern and Paula Johnson. They and our siblings shaped our lives with a love and zeal for the Lord that still vibrates in our hearts. Not a day passes that we do not thank the Lord for putting us all together as a Christian family.

Our four children have grown up to more than compensate for anything we provided. Whenever we spend time with Greg and Lynn, Kim and Ross, Kristin, or Caroline and Matt, we are grateful that the Lord worked beyond our humble efforts to prepare a new generation with devotion, skills, and creativity that push us to higher levels. As their parents, we are indebted to their love, encouragement, and generosity. We will always be standing on their sidelines to watch and to cheer God's hand of blessing on their faith and families.

Finally, when I gaze up to see the heavens at night and wonder at the vastness of our God, I always thank Him for giving me the joy of my life, Susie. If you ever meet her, you will fully understand. Her eyes twinkle with care for her family and devotion to the Lord. Her giftedness radiates, whether teaching a class or reading to a grandchild. I am humbled when I think of what she gave up to raise our family and support my ministry. Her sacrifices and labors of love are sprinkled on every page. When you use this journal and God touches your heart, be aware that somewhere Susie is praying for you. I love you, Sweetheart!

Unfortunately, the book cover only has room for one person's name; so, as you read, think of everyone who helped shape the Jesus Passages into a path for you. Our shared prayer is that you will meet Jesus in fresh ways and join us in giving all the glory to our Father in Heaven.

TOPICAL INDEX OF PASSAGES

These selected Jesus Passages will guide you to topics of personal interest. They are listed by the Passage number rather than the page number. Group leaders may use them to create a curriculum unique for their group or to answer questions that arise. Fresh ideas for using this Journal are being produced at www.readthebiblewithus.com.

ADDITIONAL RESOURCES

For more ways to use the Jesus Passages, please visit www.readthebiblewithus.com

- *Learn how to begin a group study using the Jesus Passages*
- *Find small-group lesson ideas*
- *Share your insights with others*
- *Access Ron's sermon podcasts*
- *Follow Ron's blog*

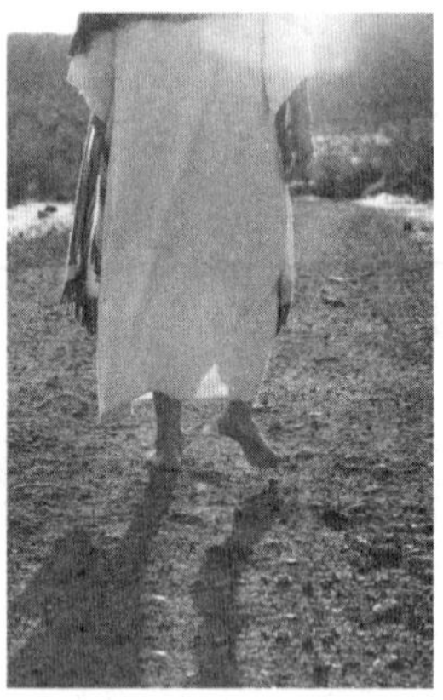

Email the author:
ron@gannettleadership.com